CAROL PURVES

From Prussia with Love

THE GEORGE MÜLLER STORY

D0238544

DayOne

British Library Cataloguing in Publication Data available

Published by Day One Publications
Ryelands Road, Leominster, HR6 8NZ
☎ 01568 613 740 FAX 01568 611 473
email—sales@dayone.co.uk
web site—www.dayone.co.uk

Designed by Steve Devane and printed by Gutenberg Press, Malta

In the preparation of this book, I would like to thank the following:
Angela, for proof reading the book, though I have drastically changed
parts, so any errors are mine and not hers;
David, for the title and checking some facts;
Fred, for checking some facts;
Paul, for his computer skills;
The George Müller Foundation, for their help and support;
and Day One Publications, for being so easy to work with.

CONTENTS

FROM PRUSSIA WITH LOVE

1805	21 October: Battle of Trafalgar
	27 September: George Müller born
1806	Britain declares war on Prussia after Franco-Prussia treaty is signed in Paris
1807	25 March: Abolition Bill against slavery
1813	Amendment of Toleration Act made an increase in missionary societies
1815	Britain, Russia, Prussia, Austria renew their quadruple alliance
1817	Gold sovereigns issued as coins
1825	November: Müller's conversion
1829	March: Müller to London
	March: Cholera in Britain
	To Teignmouth, meets Craik
1830	William IV crowned King
	August: George Müller marries Mary
1832	Invitation to Bristol
1834	Establishes S.K.I.
1836	1st home in Wilson Street
1837	Victoria crowned Queen
1841	June: Railway reaches Bristol
1847	Children still working in factories
	Cholera in Britain
1849	June: 1st home for children
1857	2nd home for children

1861	Prince Albert dies
1862	3rd home for children
1864	Clifton Bridge finished
1866	Cholera in Britain
	Craik dies
	Schooling for all by the state if not run by the church. Barnardo opens first home
1869	4th home opened
1870	5th home opened
	Mary dies
1871	George Müller marries Susannah
1875	Boy sweeps outlawed
	Begins tours
1878	Meets president of U.S.A.
1880	Every child to attend school
1881	Church of England Children's Society 1st home
1884	NSPCC formed
1887	21 June: Queen Victoria's Golden Jubilee
1892	Last tour ends
1894	Susannah dies
1897	Queen Victoria's Diamond Jubilee
1898	10 March: Müller dies

A tear-away Prussian lad

Nine-year-old George carefully pushed open the wooden door, trying not to let it creak on its hinges. As his eyes quickly scanned the study he was relieved to see no one was there. Although he knew he was alone, he still moved swiftly towards his father's desk.

A small sum of money had been carelessly left lying on the brown leather top. He eyed it eagerly. It wasn't that he had any need of it, his father always provided for him very well. What attracted him was the thrill of stealing and getting away with it. George Müller was beginning to regard himself as an expert in the art of theft.

The next problem was where to put the money. His pockets were too obvious a place; he might pull out the coins by mistake. Then he had an idea. As quickly as possible he untied the laces of his left shoe and placed the money between his sock and shoe.

He wasn't a moment too soon. Barely had he finished retying the lace, when his father strode into the room.

'George, what are you doing here?'

'Er, looking for a book, father.'

His father, an austere Prussian gentleman, glanced towards the desk.

'Where is the money that I left lying here?'

George moved slowly across the room; he couldn't walk very quickly with the coins trapped inside his shoe.

'Money, father? I didn't see any money.'

'Turn out your pockets, boy.'

Smugly, George turned out his school-boy trivia, a pen-knife, yesterday's grubby handkerchief, some polished stones and a certain amount of fluff. There was no money in his pockets at all.

'Shoes and socks off, boy.'

'But father, I haven't seen your money.'

'Off!'

As the left shoe was reluctantly removed, the missing coins rolled noisily across the polished floor.

George knew the punishment would be a severe beating, but that wasn't going to stop him stealing. He would just have to find cleverer ways of covering up his crimes.

On that day, in Prussia, Herr Müller couldn't have known that his nine-year-old thieving son would become one of the best known philanthropists of the 19th century and the benefactor of thousands of orphaned children in a far off country. But that would all be God's doing.

The 21st October, 1805, saw the Battle of Trafalgar, where Napoleon lost his fight to conquer the rest of Europe. Three weeks before this great historical event, an event of much lesser importance took place in the tiny Prussian village of Kroppenstaedt, near Halberstadt. On the 27th September 1805, a son, George, had been born to Herr and Frau Müller.

Herr Müller was a tax collector and within four years the family moved to Heimersleben about four miles away. George was to be the eldest of two sons born into the family and his father's favourite; a fact which was to undermine any good character he might have developed.

Prussia had been a nation of grandeur, royalty and nobility under a central German governmental rule. The country contained the richest of the rich and the poorest of the poor. Over the centuries deep political struggles had allowed surrounding countries to usurp their share of the land. Prussia had converted to Protestantism in the early to mid-1500s, but since that time it had become a nominal religion.

The Müllers were classed among the aristocrats. Herr Müller had strange ideas about teaching his sons the value of wealth. He gave the two boys various sums of money, not that they might spend it, but save it. From time to time he asked them if they still had the money. Invariably, George had spent some of his and then had to steal to make up the amount. It was often the taxes that Herr Müller had collected for the government that George stole. The beatings he received for this were many.

Being from a notable Prussian family, Herr Müller wanted the best education for his eldest son. Between the ages of eleven and sixteen, George was sent to the Halberstadt Cathedral Classical School in preparation for a university training. The idea was that he could train to become a clergyman and then keep his father in a comfortable way of life in his old age.

George had other ideas. He spent some time studying, but he also wasted time reading unsuitable novels and indulging in 'sinful practices'. His life of deceit and theft increased. In 1819 his father handed him some money for confirmation (it was customary for clergymen to charge a 'confirmation fee'); but when George went to the priest to confess his sins, he only handed over a twelfth of the money.

Matters grew worse.

'Have you seen my sons?' Herr Müller enquired of all he met in the town. 'Where is George? He needs to come home. His mother has died.'

George had spent the evening drinking and playing cards in a tavern until two in the morning. He had known his mother was ill, but he was too selfish to care. When he was at last discovered he was wandering the streets drunk and unable to comprehend the news he was given.

As George sobered up, he was appalled at his callous behaviour and endeavoured to improve his ways and on many evenings stayed in instead of going out drinking. But in his own strength, it proved impossible to reform.

Six weeks after his confirmation, he went to Brunswick and there became attracted to a young lady who was a Roman Catholic. With his Protestant upbringing, this friendship would bring George into further conflict with his father.

Back at the Cathedral School his wayward habits continued. He spent time playing the piano and guitar, activities which took him from his studies. His thieving continued as well. On one occasion he even stole the daily allowance of a piece of stale bread from a soldier who was staying at his lodgings. George had plenty, but the soldier would have been very hungry.

When George was sixteen in 1821, his father got an appointment at Schoenebeck, near Magdeburg.

'Could I be enrolled at the Classical School of Magdeburg?' George asked. His only reason was to try to leave his sins behind and make a fresh start.

But he wasn't really interested in any study and as he left Halberstadt it was planned that he should stay at Heimersleben until Michaelmas. He then decided he wanted to stay until Easter, even though his father insisted that he take private tuition from Dr Nagel, a learned clergyman. Sometimes George went out to collect the taxes on behalf of his father, but he still kept part of the money to spend on himself.

In November he went to Magdeburg with the express purpose of visiting his Roman Catholic young lady. He then moved on to Brunswick and for a short time he stayed with his uncle until he threw George out because of his loose behaviour.

Although he had little money of his own, George stayed at expensive hotels, hoping to impress others. When he couldn't pay at one, he moved on to another. At one hotel, when they found he couldn't pay, he was asked to leave his clothes as a security before they threw him out.

He then walked six miles to Wolfenbuttel, a charming seventeenth-century city in the heart of Lower Saxony, with a medieval castle and a number of hotels. Without any means of paying, Müller stayed at one of the hotels. When he tried to leave without paying, he was arrested and thrown into prison.

9 Pining in prison

George was horrified at the conditions in which he found himself. There were thick wooden partitions between the cells and narrow windows secured with strong bars. The food was even more of a shock.

'I'm not eating that,' he announced when presented with a meal of coarse bread, water, vegetables and no meat. 'And why am I in here with thieves and murderers? Don't you know I come from a rich and influential family?'

His jailers ignored his protests and merely took away his uneaten meal. By the second day he was hungry and reluctantly managed to eat some of the food he was presented with. In prison he was bored; there was no work and no exercise. His active mind was not being used. He became so frustrated that he even asked for a Bible to pass away the time. He also invented preposterous stories to impress his fellow prisoners. Lying came naturally to him.

He had noted that the day he was put in prison was the 18th of December. His Christmas was extremely unhappy. He was away from his friends and family; he was hungry and he wasn't sure if his father would be willing to pay the money for his release. He had to wait until the 12th of January before Herr Müller paid the necessary fine.

On learning that he was to be released, a fellow prisoner begged George to contact his sister with a message. George, in line with his fallen character, failed to contact the sister and at the time felt no shame.

Herr Müller met George at Heimersleben and took him back to Schoenebeck where he again received a severe beating. His father just didn't know what to do with his wayward son. Herr Müller thought it would be a good idea after Easter to send his son to a classical school at Halle. George stayed with his father until Michaelmas and in order to earn a little money for himself took pupils for Latin, French, arithmetic and German grammar. His father was becoming less generous.

George had heard that the discipline was very strict at Halle and was determined not to go there. In due course, he set off for Halle for enrolment, but went instead to Nordhausen, one of the oldest towns in Prussia. There, against his father's wishes, he enrolled at the gymnasium (a pre-university college) where he was to stay for two and a half years.

To cover the deception about the enrolment, George invented numerous lies, each lie becoming more difficult to sustain. When Herr Müller discovered his son had signed up for Nordhausen he was very angry, but could do nothing about it.

By now George was an extremely attractive young man, upright in appearance but not in character. He had learned to tell lies without blushing and continued to steal to provide himself with the money he needed for his wicked lifestyle. He tried to improve, but his old ways were too strong.

Müller lived at the house of the director, who was very good to him. Because of his dissipated lifestyle, George was often ill. The director's wife was especially kind to him and nursed him at these times, a kindness he was to repay with wickedness.

One day he was sent some money from his father, which he made sure he showed to everyone. He then pretended it had been stolen and ran to the director in great distress.

'Herr Direktor,' he shouted, as he ran with his coat in disarray and fear in his voice. 'My trunk has been broken into as well as my guitar case. My money has been stolen and I need it urgently to pay my creditors.'

Although the director gave George money to replace his supposedly stolen money, he and his wife never fully trusted the young man again. George's dishonesty was losing him friends and he was therefore pleased when the time came for him to transfer to Halle. He hoped to leave his old lifestyle behind, but this did not prove possible.

Müller enrolled as a student of divinity and had permission to preach at the Lutheran Establishment. The medieval city of Halle was built on the sandy plain on the banks of the River Saale. Halle University had been founded by Frederick III of Brunswick, who later became the King of Prussia. It had 1,260 students, 900 of whom studied divinity, but George later said that he hadn't heard the gospel preached and only about nine of the divinity students 'feared the Lord'.

The restrictions on his behaviour were few. Students weren't allowed to 'fight a duel' or 'molest the people in the street'. Unfortunately, there was no rule about getting into debt. To gain the money George needed, he borrowed or pawned part of his linen and clothes.

Müller's drinking was becoming legendary. One afternoon he managed to drink ten pints of beer at a sitting. About the same time he met up with Beta, a former friend from school, in one of the taverns he frequented. George was delighted because he knew Beta to be quiet and serious, with a religious faith. He thought Beta could lead him to better ways. What he didn't realise was that since the age of fifteen, Beta had backslidden and was pleased to meet George who could possibly lead him into bad society, which was what he wanted.

By 1825, Beta and George and four other friends were having various weekends away, indulging in expensive pleasures. They then decided to go to Switzerland together.

'But what can we do about passports? My father would never sign for me to obtain one,' said Beta.

'That's simple,' said George, 'we will just forge our parents' signatures. Let me have your money and I will obtain the passports.'

And that is what they did. On forged passports, the six set off and spent forty-three days in the heart of the Swiss mountains. It was more beautiful than anything they had ever seen before. On their return journey they travelled via Lake Constance and Nurenberg.

George had agreed to look after their money and pay out all the expenses. With the group's purse, he became their Judas and the holiday cost him only two thirds of what it cost the others.

In spite of all this George had not enjoyed himself and decided to go home to his father for a period. He was always searching but never finding the happiness he was looking for. He tried to reform his ways, but knew that when he was with his fellow students again, all his bad behaviours would return.

Back in Halle, one November Saturday afternoon in 1825, Beta and George were out for a walk.

'What shall we do this evening? Where shall we go?' asked George.

Beta hesitated before he replied, 'I've been in the habit of going to the house of a Christian where they have a meeting each Saturday evening.'

George was amazed, asking, 'What do they do there?'

'They read the Bible, sing, pray and read a printed sermon.'

'I want to come.'

'No, George, I don't think it's your sort of thing. You would rather be having fun.'

'No, I definitely want to come.'

George hoped in his heart that it was what he had been searching for. Then he wondered if he would be welcome; he knew he had a bad reputation in the city. Without much difficulty, he managed to persuade Beta to take him along that evening.

Going to that little meeting on a cold November evening in the heart of Prussia changed George Müller's life for ever. Consequently, the lives of many in the distant country of England would never be the same.

Missionary to where?

All together, it was a small group of about six young men, which later increased to twenty. They read the Bible together. George had been in the habit of studying Voltaire and Cicero, but the Bible was one book he had not thought necessary to study. He didn't even possess one of his own; he had to borrow one.

The group sang a few songs, the words of which seemed to be coming from their hearts. The prayers were led by a Frederick Gottlieb Kayser and were a revelation to Müller. Kayser prayed as if he personally knew the God he was speaking to. George was only familiar with the set prayers of his church, where he usually took no notice of the words that were being said. Kayser could have had no knowledge that at the small meeting was a student whom God was going to use so mightily.

George was deeply impressed by the praying. From the man's manner of speech he knew he was moderately illiterate, yet his prayers seemed more genuine than his own. He later said to one of his friends, 'I could not pray so well, though I be much more learned.'

Kayser was to have a very interesting future. In 1828 he was appointed by the London Missionary Society to become a missionary in Southern Africa. After arriving in Cape Town he pushed on to found a new station on the Keiskamma River. In 1836 he moved up river to a more suitable place and started a station called Knapp's Hope. In 1846 the Kaffir War broke out and for a while he had to move to the Kat River before he returned to Knapp's Hope in 1848. He died in 1868.

Attending this little meeting for the first time, Müller knew that it had been necessary to use a printed sermon, as it was forbidden by law in Prussia to preach if no ordained clergyman was present.

Walking home George said to Beta, 'In spite of all the wonders we saw in Switzerland and our former pleasures, they are nothing to what I have experienced this evening.'

Although George had been apologetic about gate-crashing the meeting, he was told, 'You are very welcome; my house is open to you. Come as often as you wish.'

George took Kayser at his word and returned four times during the next week and was still eager to attend the meeting the next Saturday evening. Slowly he began to realise his wickedness and abstain from his sins. He read the Bible, stopped going to the taverns and refrained from telling lies. It was his habit of lying that he found most difficult to give up and on occasions he would realise that he had told yet another lie.

Müller had always thought that it was by trying to become a better person that one became a Christian. Until this time he hadn't realised what was necessary was a personal acceptance of Christ, not his own endeavours. Müller now had this personal revelation of God.

In November 1825 he found peace with his God, but it was not until July 1829 that he made what he referred to as a 'full surrender'. He now frequently read missionary papers and began to think he was being called to be a missionary himself. His former friends mocked the change in his behaviour, saying, 'Where is the George Müller of deep drinks and madcap adventures? George Müller's now become a saint.'

But being a very new Christian, Müller was easily distracted. He was a tall, upright, handsome young man of twenty. At the Saturday evening meetings he became friendly with a young lady. He had reason to believe that her parents would not allow her to marry a missionary and therefore George's determination began to waver. In addition to this, he knew his own father would never give him permission to follow that way of life. Herr Müller asked of his son, 'Is all the money I spent on your education to be wasted?'

Realising that Herr Müller was opposed to his son becoming a missionary, George made another big decision. He would no longer sponge off his father for money. This left him with a problem. How could he survive financially? He took to heart Psalm 34 verse 9, 'There is no want to them that fear Him.'

In the future he would have to earn his own money.

Dr Tholuck, a Christian professor at Halle University, was a renowned evangelist. He was revered in America and England and in addition was so interested in the welfare of children that he had set up an orphanage in Berlin. Tholuck also took a keen interest in the student's activity in the university.

He arranged for Müller to teach German to several American gentlemen. The money earned by this teaching meant George was able to be self-sufficient. Müller was beginning to learn that God's timing was always perfect.

The question about his future still hung over him. He decided to resolve the decision by a lot. He bought a ticket in the royal lottery. If he won, he would take it as a sign that he should go ahead and become a missionary. When he did win some money on this lottery, he applied to the Berlin Missionary Society, who did not accept his application.

It wasn't until later that he learned that this was not the way God worked. It took him some time to learn this lesson, but he found that 'God would supply all his needs'; there was no reason to resort to chance or luck. He never again made decisions by using a lottery.

During this time he was not idle. He worked as a temporary chaplain in a newly established workhouse for men convicted of minor offences. Because of his past he felt well qualified for the position. In addition to work, studies, and teaching commitments, much of his time was spent circulating missionary papers. He wanted to share with others the discovery he had made about God. Wherever he went he carried tracts with him. At one period, he visited a sick man for thirteen weeks and spoke to him about his soul. Eventually the man became a Christian himself.

In 1826 Müller was asked to preach his first sermon. He agreed and during the next week committed a sermon to memory. On the 27th of August at 8.00 a.m. he gave this sermon to the congregation. He recited the same sermon at 11.00 a.m. Although he wanted to share his knowledge of God, he was unhappy with the result.

In his eagerness, he volunteered to preach again in the afternoon but had no new sermon he could learn, nor the time to do so. He felt led to expound from the text in the fifth chapter of Matthew, verse 3, 'Blessed are the poor in spirit'.

As he preached, he felt he had the attention of the people. His words were alive and with power. In the future, he resolved always to preach from the heart and not from the cold words written by another hand and memorised.

Another of the influences in Müller's life at this time was A. H. Franke. Franke had been a leading light in the 'Pietist' Movement, which had helped to purify the Lutheran Movement. He became Professor of Theology and Divinity at Halle University and before he died in 1727 had established an orphanage for 'ragged children' in the city. This orphanage, with a Day School as an auxiliary, supported hundreds of poor children, giving them 'scriptural instruction and physical benefit'.

In 1827, Müller lodged free for two months at this Orphan House. As he stayed at the house and assimilated its ethos, he had no way of knowing what a great influence this contact would have on his future life.

Still, Müller found himself sometimes slipping back into his old life. With one of his American gentlemen he went to an opera. While he was there he felt ill and in the second act actually fainted. A Christian friend said to him, 'When you fainted at the opera last night, I thought what a terrible place to die.'

The comment made Müller do some serious thinking.

In August of that year, he heard that the Continental Society wanted to send a missionary to Bucharest. This time George prayed about the matter and surprisingly his father gave his consent.

To complicate his decisions further, he heard through Dr Tholuck of a vacancy with the London Society for Promoting Christianity among the Jews. He had been studying the Hebrew language and wondered and prayed if this should be where his future would lie. He was still waiting for a reply from the Continental Society, but by further praying realised that his heart was with the Jews.

While wrestling with the problem of which missionary society to work with, news came that because of the war between the Turks and Russians the Continental Society decided it was not wise to send another missionary to Bucharest. The choice for Müller had been made.

To become a missionary to the Jews he would need to go to London for six months to train as a probationer. He wasn't too happy at becoming a student again but was able to accept the leading from God.

Just at this time, another problem arose. In Prussia every male subject had to serve as a soldier for three years. Müller had been medically examined at the age of twenty, but declared unfit. His dissipated way of life had taken a toll on his health.

Now at the age of twenty-three he knew he was in better health and likely to pass the medical. There was no way he would be able to get a passport out of the country until he had served his time or been exempted by the King of Prussia himself. He applied but no exemption was granted.

In August 1828, he was offered a teaching post in Berlin with an American gentleman who wished to learn German. Müller decided that by living in Berlin he would be nearer to the king and have a better chance of exemption from the army.

In January 1829, he offered himself for military service again and expected to start at any moment. This time he was refused as it was discovered he had a tendency to tuberculosis and was given complete dismissal for life. It was for him a time of thanksgiving. His period in Berlin hadn't been wasted as he had grown spiritually and had been able to help others. Müller was always anxious to share with others the joy he had found himself.

On the 3rd February 1829 he started his journey for London. He went first to his father's house to say good-bye. It was going to be difficult to leave his home country and family. When he arrived in Rotterdam the ice had only just broken on the river. With various delays he did not reach London until the 19th March.

Introduction to England

As Müller sailed into the London docks, he stood on the deck of the ship in amazement. He was looking at what was then known as the most advanced city in the world.

'Oh, Lord, show me your will for me in this strange country,' Müller prayed as he looked at the sights around him. Later he walked round the city taking in the views of Buckingham Palace, St Paul's Cathedral and the newly gas lit streets. It was so different from his Prussia.

It wasn't just that the sights were different. The nation was different. England was a distressed, complex country. The British were proud of their military and naval glory, but socially there was intense misery, degradation and a spirit of revolution. The evangelical spirit in the Church of England was flourishing, but much work was needed among the poor and needy.

Müller was a young man who attracted attention. He was a level-headed, earnest and thoughtful young Prussian. Nothing could disguise the fact that he was a stranger in a foreign city. Everywhere he went he stood out as a foreigner. There was a difference in fashion, food, and habits.

He found English a very difficult language to study, even though he heard it spoken every day. At the marketplace he often felt at a loss, surrounded by an unfamiliar tongue spoken at a rapid pace.

He had his first chance to witness to a young farmer that he met.

'Young man, what is the condition of your soul?'

Either his pronunciation was very poor or the farmer was offended. Müller received no response.

Not one to be deterred by difficulties, Müller plunged into his studies. While other students were having instruction in Latin, Greek, French and German, Müller was hard at work learning Hebrew, Chaldee and the Rabbinic alphabet. He found English difficult to learn; little did he realise that for most of his life it would be his constant language.

Through his connection with the London Jews' Society, Müller linked up with the flourishing evangelical section of the Church of England. It was also in this period that he heard about an Anthony Norris Groves, a dentist in Exeter who had given up his work to become a missionary. Groves believed the literal truth of the Bible, especially the verse which said in Matthew 19 verse 21, 'Sell all that you have and give to the poor.'

At first Groves gave a tenth of what he had to the poor and then he increased it to a quarter. Finally he'd stopped saving for the future and began to rely solely on God. He went to college at Dublin to train as a minister in the Church of England. It was while he was there that he came under the influence of the Plymouth Brethren.

Groves had come to believe that ordination was not a necessary qualification to becoming a missionary and therefore was rejected by the Church Missionary Society. It was in June 1829, soon after Müller had arrived in London, that Groves, his wife, and children, through the Jewish Society, went out to Persia.

Müller was very impressed with this dedication to the calling of Christ. He recorded it in his diary and even wrote to his friends back in Germany about the man. He didn't fully realise the impact the man's story had made on him.

Never one to do things by halves, in May 1829 Müller was soon ill through overwork. He felt that he was dying and even looked forward to departing this life and meeting his Master.

'You are not ill unto death,' his doctor told him. Müller felt quite disappointed but accepted the fact that the Lord still had work for him to do.

His friends advised him to have a break in the country and arranged for him to go to Teignmouth in Devon. The tranquillity at this small seaport was exactly what Müller needed. Away from the hustle and bustle of the capital, his health began to improve.

Only a few years previously a bridge had been built across the River Teign, which led to the smaller village of Shaldon. It was here that Müller got to know the Scotsman, Henry Craik. Craik, the youngest son of a clergyman, had also been converted while he was at university. After studying philosophy and divinity at St Andrews, he became unhappy with the established church. Therefore he moved south and became a private tutor to the Groves family who lived in the area of Teignmouth. It was the church he had become disenchanted with, not God. He held the Bible as the sole authority on God and once stated, 'Through my intense study of the Scriptures, I have come to believe it is a sufficient source of spiritual growth.'

Many years later Müller was able to write as testimony to this great man, 'Whilst endowed by God with such great mental powers, he did not use them to get a name among men, nor to be admired, but to throw light on the Holy Scriptures and to set forth the truth.'

Craik wrote of himself, 'I am nothing, have nothing, can bear nothing and depending on myself is madness. My depending on the Lord is heavenly wisdom.'

With beliefs like that, it was no wonder that for thirty-six years Müller and Craik were to become life-long friends and co-workers.

Müller returned to his studies in London but soon came into conflict with the society. He wanted to preach the gospel to everyone.

'Mr Müller,' he was told, 'you are being trained to preach to the Jews, not to non-Jews.'

Müller protested, 'The gospel is for all. It says in the Bible, "Go into all the world and preach the gospel." I must tell all I meet. I must continue to distribute tracts and share this good news.'

'Your primary training is for the Jews, this is where your work must lie.'

Müller realised that if he worked for the Society, his preaching would be restricted. He knew in his heart that he could not be true to their primary aims. He experienced a feeling of guilt as it was through the Society that he had been able to come to England. He offered to work for them for free but this suggestion was not acceptable. He had no choice but to offer his resignation.

Not knowing what to do or where to go, he returned to Teignmouth, where the Ebenezer chapel had just been reopened.

He started to preach in the chapel and to his intense joy one lady was converted during his first week, but he was not welcomed by all. Some of the men who preached in the chapel did not like his style of preaching and wished him to move on. Müller later commented, 'Satan knew that my preaching would be blessed in Teignmouth and therefore opposed me.'

After Müller had been preaching for twelve weeks, he was approached to become their minister at a salary of £55 a year. With a salary like that Müller knew he would not so much be 'living by the Gospel' as 'starving by it'. The decision he had to make called for a special time of prayer; when he felt sure that God wanted him to be in that place, he accepted.

Müller did not only preach at Ebenezer, he also started visiting the chapels in outlying villages. Müller preached once a week at Exeter, once a fortnight at Topsham and sometimes at Shaldon, Exmouth, and Bishop's Teignton. He began to receive invitations to preach at other village chapels in the area—Chudleigh, Collumpton, Newton Bushel, to name just a few.

Müller found the scenery in Devon so different from his childhood Prussia. He'd been brought up in cities hundreds of miles from the sea. In Devon, a county only seventy-five miles from north to south, the sea was never far away. Although a busy man, Müller could watch the fisherman at work on their nets or spy the little boats in the early evening as they put out to sea to fish all night. He thought of Jesus preaching to the fishermen.

As he travelled through the rolling countryside, he caught sight of the thatched cottages nestling round the village green, or the farm houses in the corner of the grain-filled fields. His heart thrilled as he saw the rising hills beyond. Müller remembered that Jesus had travelled from village to village preaching. He was following in his master's footsteps.

Above all he thanked God for placing him in such a beautiful place where he could tell others of his love for God and his saving grace. He knew the spiritual fields were 'white unto harvest' and he wished to be part of the gleaning.

In May 1830 Müller reached a spiritual impasse.

'Mr Müller, what do you think about adult baptism?'

'I was baptised as a child,' he replied. 'That is sufficient.'

'Have you studied what it says in the Bible about the subject and prayed about the matter?' His questioner was persistent.

Müller felt he had been put in his place. He read and prayed. Before long he too came to the conclusion that baptism by total immersion was the only way. Along with some of his friends, he was baptised by Henry Craik.

By that time Müller's form of worship was similiar to the Plymouth Brethren's. Instead of having communion once a month, he celebrated it every week. He also adopted an open type of worship where any brother could take part or preach according to his particular gift.

Big changes were ahead for Müller. When he had been studying back in London, he had been given a contact of a Miss Paget, a well-known Christian lady who lived in Exeter. For three weeks he carried this name in his pocket, without making any effort to visit the lady. When he did at last visit, she gave him an address where he might continue to stay while in Exeter—with a Mr Hake, a local school teacher.

Mr Hake's wife was an invalid who was looked after by a Mary Groves. It transpired that this Miss Groves was the sister of the dentist Anthony Groves, of whom Müller had heard while he was studying in London with the Society.

George Müller was by this time nearly twenty-five years old. He was a tall, upright, good-looking gentleman, with a fascinating German accent. Many in his congregation were secretly in love with him and mothers made plans.

George reasoned with himself that the time had come for him to be married. As a preacher it would be easier as he visited his parishioners. For quite a while he had been praying about his choice of wife. He knew the decision must have the approval of God.

As soon as Müller met Mary he was attracted to her. She was a quiet, sober, hard-working young lady. She had had a good education, played and painted and had knowledge of astronomy, history and French.

More and more George found excuses to preach in Exeter so that he could get to know Miss Groves better. Mary was equally attracted. But then Müller began to think. It would not be right to take Mary away from caring for the frail Mrs Hake. In spite of his reservations, he proposed to Mary.

On the 15th August Müller proposed, and then he was away from Exeter for four days. It was an anxious time. He supposed Miss Grove might turn him down, but when he returned on the 19th of August, he could tell by her face that the answer was to be 'yes'. They fell down on their knees and thanked God.

Once the engagement was announced another housekeeper was found for Mrs Hake. This freed George and Mary of any guilt and on the 7th October, 1830, they became man and wife.

In the marriage register George signed himself as 'George Miller', no doubt because this reflected most accurately the pronouncement of his name. It was a change that did not persist, however. When he became a naturalised Englishman on the 18th December 1861, he was again calling himself Müller and as one commentator remarked, 'George Müller was a man who never appeared to be in a hurry and always took time to place the two dots over the second letter of his surname.'

The marriage of George and Mary was not a fashionable affair. There were no orange-blossom wreaths, carriage and pair or showers of old boots as was the custom of the day. The young couple walked quietly to the church for the ceremony and afterwards had a meeting of Christian friends at Mr Hake's house. In the evening the pair drove off in the stage-coach to Teignmouth. The next day George Müller was back at work.

Theirs was to be a long and happy marriage. While Müller had a stern exterior due to his Prussian upbringing, Mary was a loving and caring lady. Together, they made an ideal couple.

West Country witness

Within a month of being married, Müller and his wife felt that it was not right to continue to accept a salary from a congregation who were very poor themselves. George reasoned that if God could provide every need, he would surely be able to provide Mary with all the necessities.

When Müller announced the decision to the church, he quoted from Philippians chapter 4, 'My God shall supply all your need according to his riches in glory by Jesus Christ.'

A box was placed by the chapel door, stating 'offering for Mr and Mrs Müller'. In the future they would pray and accept the fact that if money was not forthcoming, then it was because they did not need it. It was a decision they never regretted. The Müllers would live by 'faith'.

The box in the chapel sometimes contained sufficient money, sometimes it was almost empty. It was supposed to be opened once a week, but occasionally the steward forgot. George noted that by the 18th November, their money was down to eight shillings. Every morning Müller and his wife prayed for God to provide. Each provision from God was a miracle, but Müller sometimes was slow to recognise it.

One day George was visiting a Christian sister at the nearby village of Bishopsteignton. 'Do you want money?' she asked.

'I will only ask God for it,' Müller replied.

'But he has asked me to give it to you,' she said and gave him two guineas.

Time and time again this kind of story was repeated. Money was given to them when their need was greatest.

They never asked but people were insistent in giving. One person put money into Mary's bag while she was not looking; another placed a sovereign in Müller's pocket and then ran away.

It was rumoured that sometimes the Müllers went hungry, but George recorded, 'Never did the Lord fail.' They were never in want.

At this time Müller was not always a fit man. For some time he was dangerously ill with a gastric ulcer. He broke a blood vessel in his stomach and lost a considerable amount of blood. Again, his former life style was catching up with him. A great deal of prayer was offered for his recovery.

The year 1832 was to prove an eventful year for the Müllers. On the 8th April, after he had been at Ebenezer for two years, he wrote in his diary, 'I do not believe that we shall be much longer in Teignmouth.' This feeling was to prove true.

A noted preacher of this time, Robert C. Chapman, was being used by God to make great changes in Müller's life. Although Chapman visited Teignmouth in 1829, it is not known whether the two men actually met at this time, but as the years went by they were to become firm friends. Müller was able to share with Chapman many of his spiritual problems.

George's great friend and fellow Christian in Devon was Henry Craik. Müller records in his diary that he was attracted to Craik because of his 'warmth of heart towards the Lord'.

Craik was also noted for his absentmindedness. It was not unknown for him to be walking along in the rain carrying his umbrella under his arm. He was a man who overworked for his Lord, which meant he undermined his health and was often unwell.

This young man had been a tutor in the Groves family. When the Groves went to Baghdad, Craik had moved to another family and in April 1831 become pastor of the Sheldon Baptist church. There he had met and married Mary Anderson, but sadly she died of tuberculosis only five months later.

Craik came under the influence of Chapman and through the promptings of God moved to Bristol to preach there. Once in the city, Craik soon settled down as he became the pastor of the newly-opened Gideon chapel where attendance numbers grew rapidly and before long he married a Miss Howland.

On the 13th of April he wrote to Müller, inviting him to help with the Gideon chapel in the city. The two men had worked together very well in Teignmouth and now this godly man was inviting Müller to work with him again.

When Craik moved to the city, Müller felt keenly the loss of his friend.

Henry felt that there was future work for Müller in Bristol and asked him to pray about it. Müller did indeed pray hard about this next step in his life; he couldn't afford to move outside God's will.

Later in his diary Müller was able to state, 'I am at peace.'

The decision had been made; now he had to break the news to the chapel.

'Under God's guidance I shall be leaving the work here and moving with my family to Bristol,' Müller announced to the Ebenezer congregation.

There were many tears, some his own, on the imparting of his news. But he had to remind them that he had only agreed to stay while it was the Lord's will. Now it was time to move on.

On the 25th May, knowing that he was obeying God's command, Müller left Teignmouth with his wife and Mr Groves his father-in-law. When he said goodbye to the folk at the tiny Ebenezer chapel there were further tears on both sides.

Müller joined Craik in Bristol when it was first becoming well known. Isambard Kingdom Brunel was constructing the Great Western Railway with its terminus at Temple Meads, and the S.S. Great Britain was launched, which was the world's first propeller-driven iron ship.

In Bristol another bridge was being built, this time over the River Avon. The name of Bristol was to become synonymous with the Clifton Suspension Bridge, but when the Müllers arrived in the city, the bridge was far from completed.

Bristol had been the second port in the country, after Liverpool, but fog and sandbanks were affecting its popularity. Meanwhile the completion of the Great Western Railway meant the city was being linked with the rest of the country.

Around the year 1800, the great Brunel had dammed the River Avon to provide floating docks for the city. What was not at first realised was that raw sewage was floating into this dock and becoming trapped. A great deal of disease was being caused in this way. No wonder there were outbreaks of typhoid and cholera.

Nothing could alter the fact that Bristol was a city and therefore had its full share of poverty, unemployment, disease and degradation. There would be plenty of work for Craik and Müller.

George looked in vain for suitable lodgings and it was eventually agreed that the Müllers would live with the Craiks. It was decided that in Bristol they would all lodge with Henry Craik, his wife, and father-in-law. It was a house in Wilson Street at the rear of a chapel and belonging to it. It was only a small house, which became even more crowded when on the 17th September 1832 baby Lydia was born to the Müllers.

It was a difficult birth and Mary nearly died. Fortunately, the baby thrived, but for the rest of her life Mary never regained her full strength.

Bristol was now home for the two men and their families and was to be so for the rest of their lives.

It was not the best of times to be living in Bristol. From June to October, cholera raged in the city and the death toll was very heavy. Müller felt haunted by the sound of the funeral bell, which was ringing almost constantly. He had never witnessed death on such a large scale and was emotionally disturbed by it. He felt his own death could be near and recorded in his diary, 'Except the Lord keep us this night, we shall be no more in the land of the living tomorrow.'

But God was good; only one member of the Gideon congregation died through the disease. In addition, although the two men were continually visiting the sick and dying, they didn't catch the illness themselves. Prayer meetings were held every morning until the epidemic had spent itself.

While ministering to the needs of the congregation at the Gideon chapel in Newfoundland Street, the two men learned of a Bethesda chapel in Great George Street which was lying empty. A local Christian agreed to pay the rent on the building for a year, if Müller and Craik would reinstate it as a place of worship. On the 6th July, 1832, they began to preach at the Bethesda chapel.

Craik and Muller soon settled down to the work in Bristol, preaching at both the Gideon and Bethesda chapels. At Gideon there were some restrictions laid down by the trustees, whereas at Bethesda there were no such limitations.

Craik was probably the better preacher of the two but Müller had a following of his own. The preaching of a foreigner in Bristol attracted attention. It was not always the quality of his preaching which was the draw, but his form of delivery.

'I'm going to hear the preacher with a funny accent. He pronounces some of his words in a strange way. I want to hear him just for a laugh,' said a young Bristol lady who was looking forward to an evening of fun.

She went along to the meeting and through Müller's preaching she was convicted that she was a sinner and confessed her sins to God. George smiled when he heard the story; he never thought that his poor pronunciation could be used in that way.

For four years the Müllers had been praying for all their financial needs, without accepting a salary. God never let them down and continued to answer their prayers. The stories Müller related in his diary are numerous.

By June 1833, Müller was beginning to provide bread for hungry children and adults if they were willing to listen to Bible teaching too. Then Mrs Müller, taking as an example the Biblical character, started a Dorcas Group so richer people could make clothes for the destitute.

In the area of Bristol, George had started Day Schools, Sunday Schools and Adult Day Schools, circulating the Scriptures and helping missionaries. All this was with the idea of training and teaching others in the ways of the Lord. In March 1834 he felt he should streamline this training. He commenced the Scriptural Knowledge Institution for Home and Abroad, now fortunately known as 'S.K.I.'

Being a very methodical man he drew up seven principles and three objectives for the Institution. In accordance with his day, these were very wordy but all based on Scripture.

It was a continual struggle to find suitable staff for the Day and Sunday Schools. Only suitable people with a love for the work and for the Lord could be entrusted with this task. Theirs would be a special area of responsibility in the training of others.

An increasing workload

O n the 19th March, 1834, a son, and a brother for Lydia, was born to the Müllers. Elijah, as the little lad was christened, was a weak baby and not destined to be with them for long.

The Craiks' home was now overcrowded. They had one child and the Müllers had two. As the house was not large enough for the two families, George started to look for a place of his own. Helped by gifts of money, which he had been given towards this purpose, in May 1834, the Müllers moved to No. 6 Wilson Street in the area of High Kingsdown.

The house was built in the reign of William the Fourth, the then present king. It was not old but the architecture was unpleasant to look at. Nine steps lead down to a semi-basement that served as the front room and the best room in the house, but it could hardly be described as a breakfast room. Above were another two storeys. The brick gateway was already crumbling when the Müllers moved in.

As compensation, there was a small garden at the rear, which Müller was able to use for prayer. Nevertheless, it was their home, and as always George was most thankful to God.

Müller recorded, 'Today May 15th, we moved into our house, having lived nearly two years with brother and sister Craik.'

Through his precise Prussian upbringing Müller was a most methodical man. He was always able to quote numbers. In his diary he records at this time that the Bethesda chapel had continued to grow and membership had reached 125 and the Gideon chapel numbered 132. Both men realised it was not numbers that counted, but souls; many had already been converted by their preaching.

It seems strange to our modern eyes that the Sunday morning services were quaintly billed as 'half past ten forenoon'.

The care work that Müller did was also increasing. He now had two schools for boys and three for girls. These children were taught the three Rs—reading, writing and arithmetic, as well as 'knowledge of the scriptures'. These subjects would be of use to them as they were growing up and making their way in life.

Müller also ran two adult schools, two evening meetings for men and two for women. It was a time of intense training; the educational needs in Bristol were great.

Meanwhile, Mary's brother Anthony Norris Groves had returned from the East Indies to England. It was then his intention to go to Germany to recruit young men to become missionaries. He asked George to go with him as an interpreter.

Müller readily agreed to go with Groves; it was to be the first time he had returned to his home country. While he was there he had the opportunity to visit his father. Herr Müller was delighted to see his favourite son again and was amazed at the change in George. Müller had so many stories to tell and tried to impress on his father the importance of God's guiding.

In spite of Herr Müller's lack of interest in spiritual things, George still loved his father greatly. He recorded in his diary, 'A part of this morning I spent walking about with my father to see one of his gardens and one of his fields because I knew it would give him pleasure.'

George's father could not understand his son's faith and long ago had accepted the fact that his son would not be there to support him in his old age. This caused George much sorrow.

Müller was not away from England long but on returning to Bristol, he found considerable illness in his family. His good friend, Henry Craik, had been ill with a throat infection, but with careful nursing he soon recovered.

The other illnesses were more serious. Mary's father was dying. She had been a devoted daughter and as he passed from life to death, her heart was breaking; but she was equally concerned about Lydia and Elijah who both had chest infections.

With prayer and good nursing Lydia slowly improved. Elijah became worse as his infection turned to pneumonia. On the 26th June, he died.

Poor Mary had a double bereavement to cope with. The only crumb of comfort at that time was that grandfather and grandson were buried in the same grave.

For a while sadness pervaded the home of the Müllers, but in September Mary, George and Lydia went to the Isle of Wight to help regain their spirits. While he was there Müller had his thirtieth birthday. He recorded in his diary, 'I feel myself an unprofitable servant.'

Back in Bristol, Müller found time to re-read the life story of Franke. It was at Franke's orphanage in Halle that Müller had lodged for a while. Although Franke had died in 1727 at the age of 64, the stay in the orphanage had made an impression on Müller. This wasn't the first time he had read the life of Franke, but this time it seemed to be speaking to him personally.

Müller knew the desperate plight of many orphans in Bristol. He had been appalled at the sight of children begging in the streets. Although he was poor himself, he had often given them the odd coin as did many people in his churches. He was touched by the sad tales he had heard, and he knew that many of these children would resort to a life of crime or prostitution. Dickens, who was appalled at conditions in Victorian Britain, penned his now famous *Oliver Twist*, which scandalised the respectable people of the time. The law stated that no man could receive an allowance unless he was in the workhouse. The workhouses were made as uninviting as possible and soon became a national disgrace. Degradation was festering just below the veneer of respectability.

By 1835 there were few private orphanages in England. There were about eight in London and four in the Home Countries, but they were all small and unable to cope with the growing number of destitute children.

Müller was ahead of his times. In was in 1866 that Dr Barnardo opened his first home and Charles Haddon Spurgeon opened his the next year. In 1869 the National Children's Home was founded and the next year Fegan began his work. There was no provision for such children in Bristol.

Bit by bit Müller felt God was asking him to start an orphanage in the city. He argued with God. His family had little money; they were living on the 'bread line'. Although he was 'living by faith', could he ask God to give him money for destitute children?

Müller felt this problem lay heavy on his shoulders and prayed hard about it. He knew if it was God's will, he would provide. Müller reckoned that he would need £1,000 to start such a place in Bristol.

If it was God's will, he was determined to ask for no human help. He realised what a great witness it could be to God's provision. He prayed for months about the problem. This would be an orphanage where God supplied the means and the whole work would be a testimony to God's unfailing love. Being a man who never acted on impulse but on logic, he argued for and against for quite a while, even writing them down. He recorded in his diary, 'If I, a poor man, simply by prayer and faith, obtained, without asking any individual, the means for establishing and carrying on an orphan house; there would be something which might be instrumental in strengthening the faith of the children of God.' He also stated, 'This then would be the primary reason for establishing the orphan house.'

God gave him a special text at this time, 'Open your mouth wide and I will fill it' Psalm 81:10.

Müller had full faith in God as he prayed, 'If this is your will, Lord, please send me £1,000 for the work.'

On the 9th December, 1835, Müller held a meeting to lay before the churches and school workers his proposals. The immediate results were a confirmation that this would indeed be God's work.

One devout Christian lady offered herself to work in the orphanage without a salary. The next day a young couple offered not only themselves but all their furniture. Müller was amazed, but not surprised.

Then practical items began to arrive and were carefully recorded—three dishes, twenty-eight plates and three basins. Another day one jug, four mugs, and three salt stands arrived. Items came in odd quantities, only what the donor could give—four knives and five forks. Further days brought further gifts.

By May 1837 the first £1,000 had been received. Müller knew the work was of God.

Dr Barnardo would not begin his work in London, caring for destitute children, until the 1860s. George Müller began his work in Bristol in 1836. It was a different city, but the same need. Even in the 1800s there were 'Children in Need'.

The Brethren movement

Müller had never wished to become involved in church politics, his only will was to serve God and display his faithfulness. Through his connection with the Bethesda chapel in Bristol, he was drawn into the struggles of the Plymouth Brethren movement.

A group of Christians, most prominent among them, J.G. Bellett, E. Cronin, Lord Congleton, J. Parnell and later J.N. Darby, hired a hall in Aungier Street. A similar group had formed in Plymouth and therefore the group became known as the 'Plymouth Brethren'.

One of the pioneers of the movement was John Nelson Darby, a charismatic man of good education and considerable ability as a preacher in Dublin. When he came to England, there was a peaceful atmosphere in the movement for about seven years. Darby made a point of travelling round the country visiting different groups and staying with them for a period. This meant he was well known in most areas; a fact which would be to his advantage in future years.

Meanwhile, the Bethesda assembly at Bristol had a formal beginning in 1832 and over the years had expanded to a fellowship of several hundred. It was described as a 'Brethren-type' gathering.

In Plymouth, Darby had come into conflict with Mr B.W. Newton, accusing him of blasphemy, because of his teaching. Darby wrote many books about his particular beliefs, but they tended to be obscure and unclear to less educated persons. Many congregates at Plymouth were confused as to what the issue was.

Then came a period when Newton printed tracts stating his side of the argument and Darby did the same. It became a period of attacks and counter-attacks. There were even pamphlets issued under Newton's name, of which he knew nothing.

Mary's brother, Anthony, had been involved in the movement before he went to Baghdad, but when he returned to England in 1845 he noticed a certain exclusiveness and sectarianism. By way of warning, Groves wrote to Darby pointing out this trend.

The main point of difference between Darby and Newton was over Darby's system of 'dispensational' doctrines. Darby maintained that the faithful Jews of the Old Testament were not a part of the whole church of God. The Old and New Testament were to be seen as totally distinct and divided up into seven 'dispensations'.

Newton saw this as a new doctrine and could not accept it. The two men were in dispute as to the happenings of the 'last days'. Neither Müller nor Darby agreed with Newton's version of events.

Darby took the extreme step of excommunicating Newton from the Plymouth Assembly in December 1847. When Newton was forced to leave the Plymouth group, some supporters left with him.

Müller and the Bethesda group rejected Newton's heresy but were against the extreme action which Darby had taken. The problem then arose when some of Newton's followers applied to join the Bristol gathering. Müller was wisely anxious not to go against the discipline taken against Newton and with the elders questioned these people. They didn't want them to join them if they were tainted with Newton's dogma. Müller was willing to take these people into Bethesda, believing they had renounced their former views; he continued to accept believers from Plymouth.

When Darby visited Bristol, he was invited by Müller to preach at Bethesda. Darby declined, saying he 'would never go to Bethesda again because they had received worshippers from Newton's group'.

Certain worshippers from Plymouth were received into the Bristol fellowship although some members were against this. They felt that anyone who had come from Plymouth would have imbibed some of the errors.

Müller waited a few weeks before he took the matter to a church meeting. He had been hoping the problem would die down, but it was not to be.

Twelve senior members of the movement considered the whole question at a meeting in Bath and then signed a document acquitting Newton of any intention to deceive. It was felt that most of these charges were emotional and had no real justification.

The document made little difference to the problem. Although Müller had wanted no part of this strife, he was drawn into it against his will.

In June 1848, Mr Alexander, a supporter of Darby, left the Bethesda group, so although Müller and Craik had been reluctant to discuss the problem with the whole church, they were forced to do so. Darby produced a work of 60 pages long, but Müller and Craik were not willing to spend the time studying it. It was a document which was meant for church members only, but it fell into the wrong hands and was misconstrued to 'mean exactly what it did not say'.

Darby visited Bristol again and urged Müller and Craik to withdraw the document, but they were unable to withdraw what they believed to be the true and wise counsels.

Darby went on to describe Bethesda as not a proper assembly and excommunicated the whole church because they had admitted people who once had agreed with Newton.

The brethren all over England were sympathetic with Darby because he was the person whom they had got to know. Very few knew anything about Müller, who had not travelled so extensively around the country. Some supporters even tried to sow further discord by attacking the writings of Craik.

Decisions had to be made. A total of seven church meetings was held at Bethesda and it was agreed that 'no one defending, upholding or maintaining Mr Newton's views should be received into communion'.

The next summer when Darby called on Müller in Bristol, their meeting lasted less than ten minutes. Müller said much was to be settled before reconciliation was possible. Darby took this as a rebuff and left.

Feelings at this stage ran very high and the Brethren movement was split down the middle, divided into 'Open' Brethren and 'Exclusive' Brethren. Those who were against the excommunication of Bethesda were called 'Open Brethren'. Those in favour of the excommunication, which proved to be the larger section, were called 'Closed Brethren'.

All Müller and Craik wanted to do was to get on with the Lord's work. The whole problem was a hindrance. Müller refused to retaliate to the accusations and quietly continued with his work. The ramifications of these divisions rumbled on for many years.

Müller's heart was saddened. These problems had nothing to do with the ordinary man and woman in the street, who were daily striving to stave off the pangs of physical hunger. They were not interested in higher dogma; they just needed the simple gospel message. Müller knew the quarrels were confusing the common man. He wanted to get back to concentrating on the work God had given him. Gradually he was able to move away from the problem.

Orphans abound

The Müllers were now living at No. 6 Wilson Street in the heart of Bristol. It was here that he decided to house the orphans. During 1836 gifts continued to pour in and various staff offered their services. In February, one day was laid aside for the application for children. On that day not one application was received. George had prayed for gifts and money for the home, but had never thought to pray for children. He had known the need was so great, so never prayed in that particular way. After further prayer, within a month forty-two children's names had been put forward.

In most orphanages of the time, children were accepted on the number of votes received or personal recommendation. Müller gave priority to the needs of the children.

Müller's first intention was to care for girls between the ages of seven and eleven as he felt they were the most vulnerable. Very soon he had applications for infant-aged children and he set up another home, also in Wilson Street. Before the end of the year, there were about 350 children on the waiting list.

In 1837 there was a further tragedy in Bristol. Typhus fever was prevalent in the city. Although many died, only two cases were reported in the homes themselves and these children completely recovered; it was a testimony to the care and cleanliness in the home. Müller felt as if he had opened a floodgate of care in Bristol when he started a third orphan home for boys over seven.

'I need to record God's dealings with this work.'

In the early summer of 1837, Müller decided to write a Narrative describing the gifts and offers of help received and the progress of the work. Having a brilliant mind, every sentence was balanced, every paragraph compact and the writings displayed the thoughts of an alert, well-trained mind. Müller examined closely his reason for writing *The Narrative of the*

Lord's Dealings with George Müller. After prayer he realised the reason was to share with others the faithfulness of God. This narrative was written and distributed every year for the rest of his life. Müller also meticulously kept a diary, a habit he maintained until his last week on earth.

The year 1837 was momentous in the life of the country. King William the fourth died; the eighteen-year-old Victoria was the new monarch. Her reign was to be the longest in the history of England to date. Even so, Müller would still be alive to preach a lengthy sermon to mark her Diamond Jubilee in 1897.

The number of children Müller cared for increased. By the end of 1837, having also acquired No. 3 in Wilson Street, George records there were 81 in the home, as well as 320 in the Sunday Schools and even more in the Day Schools.

Müller led an extremely busy life. As well as having oversight of the children, he preached in the two Bristol chapels, visited the poor and sick, sent money to missionaries and distributed literature for S.K.I. Understandably, from time to time his health failed. He was able to retreat to places like Weston-super-Mare or Trowbridge for rest. Sometimes Mary and Lydia were able to join him; sometimes there was not enough money.

At the end of 1837 and the beginning of 1838, because he had been so busy, Müller was on the edge of a nervous breakdown. This time he had liver trouble and for many days was confined to bed. He said that one of the things that sustained him was to see the smart and well-clad boys and girls as they marched to Bethesda on a Sunday.

The doctors urged him to get away from Bristol, but there was no money. Then out of the blue, a lady sent him £15 with the advice to use it to get away for rest. There was no way she could know of Müller's need for a break. She lived fifteen miles away and didn't know that the doctor had given him the same advice.

While he was away he re-read the life of George Whitefield. This famous evangelist who had died over seventy years earlier came from a family who had changed their surname more times than Müller had changed his— Whytfield, Whitfield, Whitfeld, Whitefeld and Whitfeild. Müller only used the alternative names of Miller and Mueller. The evangelist was usually known as Whitefield, though pronounced 'Whitfield', Müller gained comfort from his readings. He re-read Psalm 68. Verse 5 seemed especially poignant to him: 'A Father of the fatherless and a judge of the widows, is God in His holy habitation.'

Müller's renewed energy allowed him to return to Bristol where he was able to say with the psalmist, 'Bless the LORD O my soul, and all that is within me bless His Holy name.'

The work continued to grow. The first legacy was received at the end of 1838. A young boy was dying. He had saved up all the money he had been given as presents. After his death 6s. 6¼d. was given towards the work.

George's missionary interest meant that he was often able to travel to Germany with missionaries who were going to that country and needed help with the language. In 1838 he went there again and took the opportunity to visit his father at Heimersleben. As on every visit, George was afraid that this was the last time father and son would meet.

As it turned out, the next death in his own family was not to be that of his father. After his return to England, towards the end of 1838, George received a communication from his father, saying: 'I regret to inform you that your brother died on the 7th October.'

Müller had never been close to his brother, but he had continually prayed for his soul. He had now lost this brother who had never understood him, or wanted to follow his way of life. Müller's brother had continued to live in a wicked way, which had contributed to his early death. From a distance, George grieved.

It was only two years later, when Müller visited his father in Germany again and this did prove to be the last time. Back in England, he learned from a half-brother that Herr Müller had died on the 30th of March, 1840. Again he grieved, this time for a father who had never understood him.

God continued to meet Müller's every need. Extracts from his diaries are a testimony to God's dealings with him. Examples shown in 1838 demonstrate Müller's complete trust in God and the power of prayer:

'September 18th—The funds are exhausted.'

'September 20th—The Lord has again kindly sent in a little. One of the labourers gave £6 3s. as she had promised.'

'September 29th—There is not money enough in the Girl's Orphan Home to take in bread. 15s. was received and divided between the three matrons.'

'September 30th—Today when we had not a penny in hand, £5 was given.'

These kinds of entries were recorded day after day and month after month. Seldom was there any money to spare, but never did God fail to provide.

As well as all his other commitments, Müller still found time to visit the sick and needy members of the two congregations. Working together with Craik, he endeavoured to visit members in their own homes and also have small groups for prayer and Bible study. It was his contention that 'an unvisited church was a feeble church'.

The Bristol churches were also 'missionary churches'. Sometimes there were as many as thirty men and women from the congregations out in the mission field.

With a total membership of nearly 400 Müller and Craik were in danger of being overworked. They had to appeal to church members to help them in caring for the needs of both congregations.

However, the church work did not always go smoothly. Müller and Craik worshipped with and preached at both the Gideon and Bethesda congregations. At Gideon it was the practice that some seats were paid for. The two men were convinced that all seats should be free. Salvation could not be bought. They felt the habit made a distinction between rich and poor, which was against the teaching of Christ.

As the Gideon fellowship could not be persuaded to change the practice, Müller and Craik reluctantly left the Gideon chapel and concentrated their efforts on the Bethesda chapel.

The Gideon chapel continued to operate until 1930 when it was finally closed. The empty building was destroyed in World War 2 and on the land today is a new development alongside the extension of the M32 motorway.

When the two men left Gideon, they took on the care of the Salem chapel, an unsanitary, uncomfortable building which belonged to the Countess of Huntington.

The childcare work flourished and the need for funds was always present. Müller continued his policy of never asking for money. He only asked God. In his diaries he recorded many instances of answered prayer.

One day 8d. was needed to provide the dinner in the boys' home. There was only 7d. in the kitty. One of the helpers went to look in the box in the girls' home. In it was found 1d. One penny had saved the situation. Hungry boys were fed.

Another day there was no bread or milk for the children's breakfast. They were sitting at the table and Müller had said grace in faith, even though there was no food on the plates. Suddenly there was a knock at the door. On the step stood their baker. 'I couldn't sleep last night and I felt the Lord was asking me to bake you some fresh bread and give it to you freely.'

That morning instead of the usual cheaper stale variety, the children had freshly baked bread.

Before they could start the meal, there was another knock on the door. The milkman stood there. He explained that his cart had broken down and he couldn't repair it until the milk had been removed. Would Müller accept the milk free of charge so he could get on with the repair job?

As the winter of 1842 approached, Müller in conjunction with Bethesda and Salem started the Employment Fund. The donations received were used to buy materials with which the unemployed believers were able to make articles for sale.

Saleable articles included knitted and linen garments, boots and shoes, umbrellas, woodwork, etc. As well as being sold locally, these items were sold through the post from a warehouse situated at No. 11 Frogmore Street. This scheme was not as successful as was expected, but even so over 9,000 items were sold and employment given to fifty people.

During some years there was sufficient money coming in for the needs of the children. In other years money was extremely short and the faith of the Müllers and the helpers was sorely tested, and 1843 was one of those years. It was at times like these that even extra prayers were sent up. George recorded in his diary that God never let them down.

Many children who came into the home were in poor health because of the life they had been forced to lead. Medical bills were high; there was no National Health Service. But God had taken that into account. A Bristol doctor offered to attend the orphans when they were ill and issue free medicine. There is no telling how much this offer was to save, nor how much money this particular doctor lost by his offer. His only thought had been to be faithful to God.

Müller visited Germany again in 1843. On each visit he was reminded of his wayward youth in Prussia and gave God thanks for eventually making his life of some account. He had no family in that country now, but it was still close to his heart. When looking at the church in his fatherland, he was saddened to realise that there were many divisions and a departure from God's Word.

Müller felt the time had come to print his narrative. But money couldn't be spared. Nevertheless, through God's providence money was specifically donated for this purpose.

In 1844, back in England, it was decided to send Lydia, their twelve-year-old daughter, to boarding school. Müller fully intended to pay the fees.

'No,' said the head mistress. 'I don't want you to pay for Lydia's fees. You need all your money for the orphans.'

'But, I insist,' said Müller, 'it isn't necessary for my daughter to have charity. I don't want her to be any different from the other children.'

The head had to give in. What George didn't know for many years was that the exact amount of the fees he paid was returned to him each term as a gift for the orphanage.

Money for the work often arrived in strange ways. One day a wealthy visitor to the home was asking many searching questions.

'Tell me, Mr Müller, does God really answer prayer?'

As she spoke Müller could hear the milk cart outside. He knew that there was no money to pay the tradesman. At any moment the matron would knock on the door asking for the money. George was afraid that publicly it would be shown that God hadn't answered prayer. He knew there was no money for the milkman.

The dreaded knock on the door arrived. As Müller was saying 'Come in,' the visitor said, 'I can see you're busy. I will leave now.'

As she left she handed Müller ten sovereigns. She was never to know that she had paid for the day's milk and as well as many other needs and had been the means of God answering prayer.

The Scriptural Knowledge Institution

In 1834 Müller felt constrained to continue his Christian work in a formal way which would give the glory to God. One of the means by which Müller wished to do this was to set in place a new missionary institution going under the name of *The Scriptural Knowledge Institution for Home and Abroad,* later shortened to S. K.I.

Before setting this organisation in motion, Müller prayed earnestly about the matter. In his truly methodical manner he set out the objects and principles.

The objects were:

1. *To assist Sunday Schools, Day and Adult Schools and where possible set up new ones.* Only believing Christians would be involved in the work and no teaching would be given which was opposed to the gospel.

(After sixty-three years, Müller was able to report that 121,683 pupils had attended the school. To all was given a teaching of Christian principles and teachers were able to record many conversions.)

2. *To circulate the Scriptures.* It was the object to sell them at reduced prices to poor people rather than give them free. Only in cases of extreme poverty would the Scriptures be given away.

(Again after the sixty-three years that S.K.I. had been in operation, Müller, who loved facts and figures, reported that distribution had taken place of 281,652 Bibles, 1,448,662 New Testaments, 21,343 copies of the Psalms and 222,196 of other portions of Scripture.)

3. *To aid the missionary effort.* It was not Müller's intention to set up another missionary society, but rather to give financial help and encourage those missionaries who were out in the field. Scores of individual missionaries benefited with monetary gifts during the following years.

(In his final report, Müller listed all the countries where the missionaries who were aided by S.K.I. lived and worked. It was a long, impressive list.)

4. *To circulate tracts.* These would be in English and various foreign

languages. (As this part of the work continued and grew Müller took premises in another part of town to store and distribute literature. This shop was to survive into the next two centuries and now stands as the Wesley Owen Christian Bookshop in Park Street, Bristol. This Edwardian street was built quickly and temporarily and was not expected to last. The room above the shop was at one time used as a flat for older girls or boys.)

(Müller recorded more than 11 million tracts had been circulated, or as he more accurately stated, 111,489,067)

5. *To start orphanages for the needy children in Bristol.* It was this object of S.K.I. which became the most well known during Müller's lifetime. Many people were willing to give money and gifts for use for the needy children, while not so willing to give to the other causes. They didn't realise that in Müller's sight all the objectives were to extend the kingdom of God.

Müller and his colleagues also set down a list of principles. They wished everything to be clear right from the start. For the list of principles, he also leaned on Scripture:

1. We consider it the duty of every Christian to be involved in one way or another in the cause of Christ (Matthew 13:24–43, 2 Timothy 3:1–13).

2. We do not wish any unsaved person to be a patron of the institution. They felt that would be dishonouring to God; he was to be the only patron (Psalm 20:5).

3. We will not ask unbelievers for money (2 Corinthians 6:14–18). If they offered money of their own accord, then it would be accepted, but never asked for (Acts 28:2–10).

4. Non-Christians will not be involved in the running of the institution. This would bring into play factors which were of the world and not of God (2 Corinthians 6:14–18).

5. No project will be started without the money on hand. No debt will be incurred. Müller even went to the lengths of paying tradesmen daily instead of weekly, in case there was no money to pay the bills at the end of the week (Romans 13:8).

6. The success of the institution will not be judged by the amount of money given or the number of Bibles distributed. That is the judgement of the world. Success will be measured by God's blessing on the work

(Zechariah 4:6). Müller was only too well aware of the fact that the more prayer was offered up, the more would be the results.

7. The institution will be run simply on scriptural lines. But advice offered prayerfully from experienced Christians will be favourably received.

Where possible, money was divided equally between all the objectives. But Müller always prayed before making any allocation; he did not wish to move outside God's direction.

To dip into the pages of the annual report of S.K.I. over the years is to have a fascinating read. The Report for 1837, which cost 4d., listed again the objects of the institution. Müller believed that a mere list of figures would be dull reading. Therefore, whenever possible, he listed the items received or the destination of the money.

The report printed in 1846 recorded—£1 for a few bricks, 5s. worth of postages, two packets of bad halfpence to be sold as old copper. Often the receipt of 'bad coins' was recorded.

The donation of 280 apples is noted next to the receipt of a flute and music stand. The next item is a corn eradicator, then two little worked mats. It is not clear whether the mats were tiny or unfinished.

The report printed in 1848 placed on the same pages all the monetary gifts, the items came later. They included such items as tapioca, gingham material, and two copies of *Harry and his Nursemaid*.

Some reports recorded the receipt of mourning rings, a common item in those Edwardian days. When sold these items of precious or semi-precious metals raised further money.

The descriptions of anonymous donors were noted—'God's Steward', 'Interest', 'Us Three', 'Two Poor Girls', 'A Welshwoman', 'Mizpah' and 'Of Thine Own Have We Given Thee', donors whose name is only known to God.

One person sent £3 and asked for it to be acknowledged in the Bristol *Evening News*, stating it was from 'An old Maid'. Müller duly did this, but a few days later the donor asked for another advertisement to be placed in the paper. Presumably she had not seen the first one. General facts about the children were included in the reports. They stated that during the year more children were received and left and nine had died. Many children left to be reunited with family relatives, some to Christian families. All left with a new outfit of clothes. The number of children cared for by 1899 had reached 10,172. Individual reports were received about missionaries out in the field. In the 1899 edition, many citations were printed about George Müller himself.

In a number of reports the list of missionaries who had received gifts were over one hundred and fifty.

The 1898 report mentioned the circulation of 285,407 Bibles, 1,459506 New Testaments, 21,365 Psalms and 222,986 smaller portions of Scripture. Mere figures, but Müller and his successors knew each item was a potential means of revealing the truth of God to the reader.

Müller realised S.K.I. had a small beginning which started so quietly and surely, but he also knew with God's help it could reach great proportions. Even he would have been surprised to know that it had touched the lives of thousands into the third millennium. There can be no knowing the great influence the institution had on the lives of many Christians, whether in England or in distant mission fields round the world. It was a great influence for good in a needy world.

In his final report, Müller stated: 'The total amount of money received by prayer and faith for the various objects of the Institution since the 5th March 1834 is £1,424,646 6s. 9½d. (Or as he even more impressively wrote in his report—one million four hundred and twenty four thousand six hundred and forty-six pounds, six shillings and ninepence halfpenny).'

Moving times

Conflict was on the way. The homes were full of noisy, boisterous children in the four houses. Wilson Street was a quiet residential, respectable road.

'Mr Müller, may I have a word with you?'

Müller sensed trouble was approaching when a resident spoke to him one morning.

'We all know what a wonderful work you are doing, but the disruption to the rest of the street is very great. It would really be better if you moved somewhere else.'

There was further bad news.

'We have also been having trouble with the drains. These houses were not built for so many people.'

Müller knew the truth of what the man was saying, as a shortage of water had always been a problem with the needs of so many children. But where could they move? They were only just surviving financially in Wilson Street. He had a very urgent need to pray about it. In his most businesslike way he wrote down the reasons for moving and the reasons for staying. The reasons for moving were many and compelling.

As had been pointed out to him, living near so many children would be a wearing experience. He knew he himself would find it disruptive to a quiet existence. As had also been pointed out to him, the drains could not cope with the quantity of water being used. There was only one proper playground for the children, so each house had to take its turn to play.

Müller considered the option of buying and building on a plot of land. The ground around the building could be cultivated and the boys could be employed doing this. In Wilson Street, there was no suitable outlet for any activity for the boys. Larger buildings would mean all the washing could be done on the premises and the girls could be trained in this matter, which would give them preparation before they went out into service.

Furthermore, pollution was high in the centre of Bristol where they were positioned. The children needed better air in the hills around the city. The teachers had nowhere to relax and there was no place to isolate sick children.

There were many good reasons to move, but where and how? The idea of building an orphanage began to grow in Müller's mind.

As well as praying, he consulted his good friend Robert C. Chapman whose reply was, 'You must ask help from God to show you the plan, so that all may be according to the mind of God.'

Müller knew that if the move was of God, money would be forthcoming. He decided first to pray for a piece of land so that he could build an orphanage to house all the children who were in need in the city.

A plot of six or seven acres would be needed, which cost around £3,000 and for the erection of the building, at least £8,000.

On the 10th of December, 1845, the first £1,000 was received as a gift. On the 30th of December another £1,000 was received. Müller took all this as a sign he should press on with the work.

'I know of a Christian architect who will design the building at no cost to yourself,' Mary's sister announced when she heard the plan to build.

The next thing for Müller to do was to find the suitable plot of land just outside Bristol. He viewed several unsuitable places. Then on the 2nd February, 1846, he recorded the amazing news, 'Today I heard of suitable and cheap land on Ashley Down.'

He knew this to be a suitable area. Only a few miles away from Wilson Street, the air on the Down would be clear and fresh and it was surrounded by fields where the children could play. The land which had views in every direction was near to the Bethesda chapel. This would be another advantage.

The following day he noted in his diary, 'Saw the land. It is the most desirable of all I have seen.'

The seven acres were on offer at £200 per acre, but the owner was willing to sell to Müller at £120 for each acre. He calculated a saving of £560, a great deal of money to Müller. By the 5th of February he had purchased the land.

Müller's next task was to wait until enough money had been received to start the actual building. He was not prepared to begin until the money was in; he didn't intend to be in debt.

Müller felt alone and hesitant. Only occasionally did he consult other Christians for advice; on most occasions he relied solely on God. He was sometimes criticised for this attitude and it meant he often ploughed a lonely furrow. He now felt hesitant; it was a very big step.

Then the gifts of money started arriving in small and large amounts. The small amounts were no less precious: £2 from a member of the Gideon chapel, 6s. 4½d. from a widow, 10d. from a lad who had sold scrap, £100 from a wealthy businessman. The gifts were many and varied.

In his careful way Müller recorded that there was £9,285 3s. 9½d. in the building fund and on the 5th July, 1847, building was able to commence. So trusted were the builders and so particular Müller's instructions that for the remainder of the year he was able to be away on a teaching and preaching tour in Westmoreland and Cumberland.

In the midst of all his planning for the building, Müller had a further happiness in 1846. Lydia, now fourteen, had always been a serious young lady who attended to her studies well. But the whole family knew that she wasn't a Christian just because her parents were. Towards the end of that year, Lydia was able to accept Jesus as her own Saviour and was baptised and received communion. Her faith would sustain her all her life.

During the next year, the building work continued steadily. There were about 130 people in the four homes in Wilson Street. The new building was urgently needed.

It was recorded that £15,784 18s. 10d. had been received in gifts and £2,000 for furnishings. All these gifts were being received at a time when the financial condition of the country was in a difficult position. In 1846 the wheat and potato crops had failed, bread had become twice the price of the previous year and the amount of potatoes Müller had to purchase was taking a larger percentage of the money. But God was faithful.

'Today's the day. We're moving.'

'Matron says there will be room for us all to play at the same time.'

'She says you can see all of England from the hills.'

'No, not all of England, just some of it.'

The children themselves were so excited when the time came for them to move. Gathering up their few belongings they could hardly wait for their turn.

It actually took four days in June 1849 for all the belongings to be loaded on to carts to make the journey up the hill. The children were only too eager for their turn to arrive. Once in the building on Ashley Down they couldn't believe the size of the rooms. It felt like a palace, they had never been in such a large building. There was room for 300 people and gradually more orphans were admitted.

Müller didn't forget the Christians who had made the building of this new home possible. He carefully listed in his diary the countries from which donations had been received—Australia, East India, West Indies, United States, Canada, Cape of Good Hope, France, Switzerland, Germany, Italy and so on. Those who gave did not always realise the care and thankfulness with which each gift was received. Small gifts were just as welcome.

The people of Bristol were very interested in this new building that had gradually appeared on the skyline. They wanted to see it for themselves. Wednesday afternoons became visitors' afternoon. One of the helpers guided groups of about forty people round the building.

Visitors were amazed at the sights they saw. Instead of the emaciated children who had formerly been seen round the street, they saw well-fed industrious youngsters. They were either at their studies or working at their sewing or in the laundry or boot room.

Each child had his or her own little bed space and place for personal belongings in the washrooms. Everywhere spoke of devotion and care. Müller was demonstrating to the world God's unfailing love.

Although there were three-hundred children under his care, Müller knew that there were many more in the city. He began to pray along the lines of opening another home for the needy.

Gifts continued to flood in. Those that could not be used in the home were able to be sold to swell the funds. When Müller was given a 1535 Coverdale Bible, he sold it for £60. As well as benefiting the orphanage, some of the money was spent on large print books for the aged, as the donor had requested.

Gifts for the work continued to arrive, many with a touching story behind them. A widow of about sixty sold her house and sent the proceeds of £90 to Müller to be spent for missionary work. He was very worried that this was an impulsive act that she might regret in the future. He offered to pay her expenses for her to come to Bristol, so that they might discuss the matter.

'I made God a promise', she said, 'if ever we owned the house in which my husband and I lived, we would give it to the Lord. My husband has now died and I own the house, so I now want to sell it and give the money to missionary work.'

'But you are poor and failing in health. How will you live?' Müller asked.

'God has always provided for me and I have no doubt he will in the future. I can work as well as any other, as a nurse or anything.'

Müller was not able to dissuade her, nor make her accept her travelling expenses. To make absolutely sure, Müller kept the money for nine months and then wrote to her again. Was she sure she still wanted to give it? Would she like it all back or part of it? She had not changed her mind. Müller very prayerfully decided which missionaries should receive portions of the money.

In the midst of all the dealings with the children, death and illness were never far away. In May 1853, Mr Anthony Norris Groves, Mary's brother, died shortly after his return from the East Indies. But there was even more distress for Mary—Lydia became very ill with typhus fever. It was only after a month of severe illness and intense prayer that Lydia gradually recovered. Müller could again return his attention to the orphanage.

A million and a half in answer to prayer

This was the subtitle of George Müller's autobiography—a fitting title as much of Müller's time was spent in prayer. God was his friend to have conversations with and it was God who answered his prayers in a million ways.

Every gift received was carefully recorded. None of these gifts had been asked for directly. Money went to missionary operations, children's work, or the distribution of Scriptures and tracts.

When the Müllers began to 'live by faith', Mary and George often started the day without the financial means to meet the requirements of the day. They were living completely 'hand to mouth'. But God met each of their needs as it arose and George's diaries are full of stories.

On one day there was no money to buy food. A certain sister had sold some trinkets meaning to give the money for the orphans. On this particular day, during her prayer time, it was impressed upon her not to delay, but to hand over the £5 immediately. The lady was not to know that at this time there was no money to buy food for the children. Her gift provided the next meal.

Another widow, who was interested in the work, was being shown around by Mrs Müller. Before she left she pressed into Mary's hand two sovereigns. Again it was a day when all the money had been spent and the children had been hungry.

At one time the milkman and the baker were paid weekly. At the end of some weeks all the money had been spent on other essential items. Müller came to believe that if these bills were not paid daily, it was a form of debt and God was not being honoured. He decided in the future to pay for these items on a daily basis. Money always arrived in time, but sometimes only by a few minutes.

One week there was no money to pay for newly-baked bread. One of the workers who had been away from Bristol for a few days brought with her

£1 10s. 6d., which was found in one of the collecting boxes. Nothing was bought for which they couldn't pay at once.

Another day the matron was going to send away the baker as there was no money to pay for the bread. At the same time a lady called who had done some needlework which she had sold. She brought in the 3s. 11d. she had received for the work and again the children were able to have fresh bread. The alternative was the cheaper stale bread, which on some days had to be staple food.

Some blankets had been given to the homes. These were not needed immediately and were stored away carefully. When the matron came to look at them, the moth had got into one pair. Therefore the rest were sold immediately and the money used to buy more provisions.

A sack of potatoes had been ordered, but on the expected delivery date there was no money to pay for them. Because of delivery problems, the potatoes arrived a day late, by which time money had been received to pay for the vegetables. As the potatoes had arrived a day late it had been possible to buy bread on the previous day.

Four old five-shilling pieces were received by Müller with a note explaining that the grandmother of the donor had been given them on her wedding day. As they were the first gift from her husband, she kept them and subsequently passed them on to each of her grandchildren. These recipients realised that they were not doing any good sitting in a drawer and so decided to send them to be spent on the orphans. Over the years a great deal of money was raised by the numerous old coins which had been sent in to Müller.

Ten pounds was sent by a man whose horse had been stolen. He had made a pact with God, if his horse was returned he would give a thank offering for the work among the orphans. The horse was returned and in gratitude, the ten pounds was faithfully handed over.

Some gifts were strange but valuable because they could be sold for cash. Five pieces of artificial teeth, four of them set in gold, were sent from Buxton. Old teeth seemed to have been received on many occasions.

One gentleman sent a donation on behalf of his wife who had just died. She had been a resident at the orphanage and never forgot the kindness she had received there.

Another letter gave thanks for the 'kind and fatherly care' which the lady had received while in the home. She explained that since leaving Ashley Down, she had learned to love her Saviour.

When either boys or girls were in their last years in the homes, they were given training in a suitable trade. It was taken into account where their special aptitude lay, so that they could be as successful as possible in whatever line they chose.

In addition, all the young people were fitted out with a set of clothes. These were taken from the large stock room where donated clothes were stored.

Sometimes donations were sent because of guilt. An anonymous letter was received from Devon, stating, 'Twenty-eight years ago, I stole some money from a collecting box which was meant for your work. To make up for this deed, I now wish to pay back the amount with interest.'

As many people received Müller's annual report, they felt moved to give to the work he was doing. So many letters began with the words—'Thank you for a copy of this year's report.'

An officer in the navy, who had given up his rank to pursue Christian work, made a donation from his naval days—three silver teaspoons, three silver forks and two teaspoons. The money raised when these items were sold met the needs of the homes for two days.

A couple who were visiting the homes, commented, 'You will not be able to continue without a good stock of funds.'

They were told by the matron, 'Our funds are deposited in a bank which cannot break.'

With tears in his eyes, the gentleman handed over £5. This was on a day when there was not a penny to hand.

'Not a penny in hand' was a phrase that Müller often used in his diary. Many a morning came without the means to pay the bills for the day. By the end of the evening, with much time spent in prayer, the necessary money had been received. Never once did a bill go unpaid. God knew just when to supply the money.

Yet another gift was received anonymously. A little boy arrived with a letter from a gentleman and lady he had met in the street, with the instruction to hand it in at the house. It contained £5 with a note attached, 'Please accept for the benefit of the orphans, in the name of Lord Jesus.'

One August provisions were very low as few funds had come in and the minimum of food had been bought. The children were facing a day when they would have dinner but no tea. Some of the helpers went out to sell a few items that had been sent in and enough money was collected to be able to buy the tea. It was on more than one occasion that the ability to feed the children had been as close as that.

A large tea chest had been handed in by a brother at a period when there was no time to deal with it immediately. When it was opened and the contents sold, 15s. was raised. On that day exactly 15s. that was needed to pay for washing.

Not all gifts were suitable in the home. Four pewter dishes had been given, but had not been used as they were not a suitable size. These were sold for 9s. 6d. More necessary food was bought.

On another day when food was low, a lady sent in two dozen boys' shirts. She had made them for the homes, knowing that shirts were always needed by the boys. Along with the shirts she sent 5s. to get them washed. The helpers washed the shirts and the five shillings became the next meal.

Not all gifts were accepted. It was a New Year's Day when Müller received a sealed envelope from a lady whom he knew to be in debt. On opening the envelope, he didn't feel he should take this money. He returned the envelope and the money to the lady urging her first to pay her debts. This was on a day when there was not enough money to buy the next meal. Müller knew God would provide; it was not necessary to accept money which should be used to pay off a debt.

One sunny day, the infant children were out walking with their teacher. They were approached by an older lady. She placed twopence into the teacher's hand, saying, 'It is but a trifle, but I must give it to you.'

One of those pennies was used immediately to buy bread for the evening meal.

It was not only gifts of money that were received. The list of goods was endless—6 yards of calico, 5s. worth of postage stamps, pairs of stockings, an old sixpence and clothing for the children.

Late one night a gentleman came to Müller in his office and gave him two sovereigns. When Müller asked for his name, he replied, 'If it would be of any benefit, I would give it to you. But as it would not, simply put down in your report as "Sent", for I am sure that the Lord has sent me.'

Another donor was the person who saw the door of the house open and rolled in half a crown. The donor was never discovered, just the coin on the hall floor. This was at a time when there was nothing in hand.

The staff themselves had to make great sacrifices. Some weeks it was not possible for their wages to be paid. They too had to 'live by faith'. At other times they sold even more of their few possessions, so that the children might be fed and bills paid. Sometimes it was the helpers who went short on food, never the children. But each member of staff had been carefully and prayerfully chosen. They considered it a tremendous privilege to be allowed to help in this great work.

No money was ever asked for, but in the local churches and in the homes there were boxes into which donations could be placed. Money was often put in there secretly and often the money paid for the next meal.

Müller was never surprised to receive money at just the time it was needed. He knew that God was in control of all things and would know when the need was greatest. It was never a question of 'if' but 'when'.

George Müller never took God's provision for granted. A glimpse into his diary shows his total dependence on God in face of the need:

'August 6th—During this week I shall have to pay again £35 for the orphans and have but £19 towards it. I believe he will help but I know not how.'

'August 18th—In a day or two again many pounds will be needed. I have not one penny in hand. My eyes are up to the Lord.'

'August 20th—I gave myself to prayer this morning, knowing that I should want again this week at least £13.'

'August 31st—I have been waiting on the Lord for means, but as yet the Lord has not been pleased to send help.'

'September 1st—"the Father of the Fatherless" will send help.'

'September 5th—Our hour of trial continues still. But I have faith in God, I believe that He will surely send help, though I know not whence it is to come.'

'Living by faith' was not an easy option.

Onward and upward

In December 1850 there were seventy-eight children's names on the waiting list and by 1856 this had grown to 850. Müller was most distressed to turn even one child away. The need for a second orphanage was very great. Donations had continued to flood in and by 1855 Müller was able to have the work commenced on the piece of land adjacent to the first building. As he was living close by, it was easy for him to keep an eye on the work. The children themselves were excited as they could see the building grow each day.

'Look at that big hole. That's where the new orphanage is going to be.'

'That means more children will be able to be as happy and loved as we are.'

'More children for us to play with.'

'Haven't you got enough friends already?'

But 1852 had been a difficult year. Although Müller was close to God, he still had his trials. The killer-disease scarlet fever raged through the orphanage, affecting more than a quarter of the children. Müller was so thankful that because of the extra space they were able to isolate the sick. Still, five of them died, a sad period for all concerned.

George was still being offered donations he couldn't accept. One lady sent £100 with the note 'for you in your old age or for your wife and daughter if you die'. Müller felt it necessary to return it with his own note, writing, 'The Lord will provide. He has in the past, he will in the future.'

Of the small amount of money Müller did have of his own, he often gave to the children's work or to missionaries. Rather than resenting this, Mary would often comment, 'Thank you, my dear.'

In spite of George being so busy, they had a happy marriage. Mary laboured hard supporting her husband in the work and attending to the needs of the children. And although he had many tasks to attend to each day, he always delighted in the evenings to spend a small time sitting beside her, talking over the happenings of the day. They were intensely interested in the work that each was doing.

George and Mary had been married for twenty-nine years. She had never been in good health since the birth of Lydia and now suffered from rheumatism. Often she was in a great deal of pain. Her left side particularly was affected and because of swollen fingers she had to have her wedding ring cut off. One welcome gift which they did receive was a couch on which she could rest.

Mary went regularly to Cleveden for warm sea-baths, which slightly relieved the symptoms, but one day she slipped and fell while she was there. She had to remain in Cleveden for three months.

By 1857, the second house was nearly finished. In his faithful way, Müller accurately recorded that the building had cost £21,000 and together with Orphan House No. 1 would be able to provide for 400 children—all this by never directly appealing for funds, but waiting on the Lord in prayer. There was great excitement and rejoicing when the second orphanage was opened on the 12th November.

The orphanages were never given fancy names, just referred to as Orphanage No. 1 and Orphanage No. 2. There were now two buildings to maintain but some parts of building No. 1 were wearing out.

At the end of November, with winter rapidly approaching, the boiler which supplied all the hot water and heating ceased to work. It would take a few days to repair or replace. The children, especially the young ones, would be very cold. The boiler was surrounded by brickwork, which would have to be removed to find out the cause of the trouble.

There was no choice. It was decided to have the work commenced on a Wednesday. On the preceding Thursday and Friday a bitter north wind started to blow and the first cold days of winter appeared. Müller and the staff prayed about the matter. First, they prayed that the men would work quickly and second that the weather would not be so cold.

On Tuesday evening the cold north wind was still blowing, but by Wednesday morning it had veered to the south. The weather was so mild that no fire would have been needed in any case. As the work commenced Müller overheard the foreman say to the leader of the workers, 'I would like the men to work late this evening and come again very early in the morning.'

He was told, 'No, sir, we would rather work all night.'

Müller then remembered that he had prayed that the men would be 'given a mind to work'. The work was speedily finished and the heating restored. But Müller made sure a new boiler was ordered in the spring. The reconditioned one would never last another winter.

Not everyone was in agreement with the work Müller was doing. S.K.I. was especially criticised. One group of people made two accusations. The first accusation was that Müller was able to obtain money because he was a foreigner; the second was that the whole idea was a novelty. On both points he was able to refute their arguments. He thought being a foreigner made it more difficult to collect money and the idea was hardly a novelty as, at that time, it had been going for twenty years. He explained, 'I have no secret treasure. My only secret treasure is God.'

Poverty still raged in Bristol. Many adults were dying through epidemics and poor conditions. More and more orphans were in need of care. Müller prayed about the conditions. He reasoned that if God had provided adequate money for two homes, he would provide for three. At the beginning of 1858, Müller purchased 11½ acres of land adjacent to the first two homes. Work on the building did not commence until July 1859, as Müller would not build until he had the money in hand.

Müller was always careful about the staff he employed. Such people would be leading a life of dedication and hardship. As time went on, unlike some orphanages, there were few changes in staff. Many remained for more than a quarter of a century. When old boys and girls visited the homes they were able to introduce their children or even grandchildren to the same staff they knew.

Although Müller always made the final decisions, he was pleased to have with him men of high standing and integrity.

One such man was James Wright. He had a good Christian background, was well founded in the faith and also agreed with the principles of 'living by faith'. He had a good head for business and soon became a second-in-command to Müller. Wright had a good singing voice and could often be heard leading the choir at the Bethesda chapel.

It was 1861 and Orphanage No. 3 was nearing completion, but already Müller was starting to pray about buildings Nos. 4 and 5. The waiting list had grown to a thousand. He knew that while the need was there, and if it was God's will, he would provide the means. The first orphans were received into No. 3 on the 12th of March, 1862. The building on the 11½ acre site housed 450 children and had cost £23,000, all money never directly asked for, just provided by God's prompting to other Christians. There were now 800 children in care.

Among the many gifts which were received was £5 from a fisherman. The man had resolved that the proceeds of one night's fishing would be donated to the work. He had prayed that it would be a large catch and it was.

Sometimes twenty or thirty donations were received in one day; sometimes only £12 was received. This was at a time when the outgoings were up to £300 a day. Humanly speaking it would not have been possible to carry on with such differences in donations.

The large amount of water needed for the home was always a problem. Two- to three-thousand gallons were needed each day. They received the water from fifteen large cisterns and nine wells within the grounds. In the summer of 1864 there was a severe drought. The cisterns became empty and the wells ran dry. Two local farmers helped from their wells and water was taken from a local stream.

After this terrible summer, the British Water Works Company was able to lay pipes, thereby ensuring a permanent and unfailing supply.

To build orphanages Nos. 4 and 5, Müller looked to the piece of land on the other side of the turnpike road. He prayed, but there were many obstacles. The eighteen acres had been let out until March 1867. The owner was asking £7,000 for the land which was more than Müller was willing to pay. In addition, the Water Works Company wanted the land for a reservoir.

Slowly, the problems were solved. When the water company realised that it was wanted for a charitable work, they withdrew interest.

'Will you sell me the land for £5,000 instead of the asking price of £7,000?' Müller asked the owner.

The man gave the idea some thought and eventually agreed. In addition, the tenant agreed if he were paid compensation, he would leave early. Prayer had removed many obstacles in this case.

In March 1865 the land was paid for, the deeds were in possession and the plans drawn up. Müller then realised that it would be more convenient and cheaper to build the two houses at the same time, to the same design. This would mean a delay in commencing the work, but it was good business sense. Müller had always been a shrewd businessman.

A local glazier offered to pay for and fit all the glass in these buildings. All the money saved was put towards other furnishings.

The smallest of gifts were recorded and where possible acknowledged. A mother and daughter seamstress donated a farthing, halfpenny or penny for every garment they made during the year. This amount was recorded alongside £100 from Dublin and £250 from a missionary which was to be given to other missionaries. Much of the money was donated to others. There were 122 missionaries and labourers for the gospel who received money from Müller.

On the 3rd of May, work on No. 4 commenced and slowly but surely the holes were dug and the bricks put in place. As the children played in the grounds or made their way to and from the existing buildings they could see how the work was progressing. They were excited; they knew what it was to be rescued from poverty.

'More children,' said one child.

'More friends,' commented another.

By December the contract was signed for No. 5. Again the skyline of Bristol was being changed. From many parts of the city, the buildings could be seen. Kelly's map of Bristol for 1885 shows the buildings marked as 'Orphan Asylums'. The dictionary meaning of the word 'asylum' is 'a place of safety'. (A later Ordinance Survey map of 1902 simply marks the buildings as 'New Orphanage Homes', with many of the adjacent fields turned into hundreds of houses.)

In his diaries, Müller often quoted verbatim from the letters he had received: 'Last year I said to my husband, we will give to the Lord one of our young hens and now I enclose 1s. 8d. in stamps, the sale of her first eggs.'

In addition to organising the new buildings, Müller continued to be a regular preacher in Bristol and the surrounding area. This was a work he had shared with Henry Craik for over forty years. Indeed, Craik was probably the better preacher of the two.

In 1859 Craik had become ill with a weak heart and by 1865 was desperately ill. Like Müller he was sixty. By January of the next year he lay dying. Müller and Mrs Craik sat by his bedside. He was too ill to talk.

Müller himself became ill with a severe cold and was not able to visit. The two men were not to meet again. Craik died on the 22nd January 1866.

Müller had consulted his friend about many of his decisions and felt his loss keenly. So much so that he was unable to attend the funeral and for a while his own health deteriorated. Craik's death made George realise his own slender grasp on life.

Henry Groves, Mary's nephew, came to Bristol for a while to try to step into Craik's shoes, but Müller would never have another friend like Craik.

Donations continued to arrive. One lady had received a sum of money and decided to donate a quarter of it to the work of the orphanages. Another lady saved up 2d. a week and when she had enough, she sent the work 10s. A shopkeeper sent 3s. 5d., being a penny for each pound he had received during the previous week. All were faithfully recorded and prayerfully spent.

A Danish master of a vessel sent £10. When his ship had been battered by a southerly wind, when he was coming up the channel, he had promised God if they survived he would give the money to the Lord as a thank offering. He kept his promise.

One old lady who had worked very hard to earn her money and had sent £5 every year, left £600 in her will for the work.

A Swedish man sent £5 9s. 7d. on behalf of his brother who had just died. Together they had made some money through publishing a hymn book and the brother had always requested that on his death money should be donated to 'Mr George Müller's mission to the heathens'.

Towards the end of December 1868, Müller recorded the gift he had received from London—a gold watch and chain, diamond ring, 3 other gold rings, a gold necklet, 7 gold studs, 3 pairs of gold earrings, 2 gold breast-pins, 4 brooches, a gold cross, 2 lockets, 2 bracelets, 2 pairs of links, etc. All these items were sold to raise money for the missions.

On the 5th of November, 1869, orphanage No. 4 received 420 destitute little ones and on the 6th of January, the next year, 153 children moved in to No. 5. There were now about 900 children in care. All expenses had been met, all workers paid, and a balance left of several thousand pounds. In all that time Müller had never directly asked for funds. Money had been given by people who had prayerfully felt led to give.

Home comforts

Conditions for the poor in Victorian England were dire. Unemployment, especially in the cities, was rife. Children were often sent out to earn a few coppers wherever they could. Schooling was an option few could afford.

Food was in short supply and expensive, and because of malnutrition, the weak became weaker, and the hungry hungrier. A penny loaf of bread was a luxury. The staple diet was bran dumplings, served with 'roast', 'baked', or 'boiled' meaning roast turnip, baked turnip or boiled turnip. An alternative was uncooked turnip. There was no question of not liking turnips.

Tea was a drink which was made without tea. A piece of bread was placed in the fire until it was burnt and then put in the teapot.

As one poor labourer said, ''Taturs 'twas that most folk lived on in them days. What did we do when there were no taturs? Well, we'd to do wi'out them.'

The children who were admitted into the homes had been rescued from even worse conditions. They had lost both parents and those with relatives found they were unable to care for them. Many of the older ones had turned to crime and all knew loneliness and rejection. Anything that Müller had to offer would have been welcome, but the conditions in the homes were of an extremely high standard for the nineteenth century.

When visitors toured the homes, cleanliness and neatness was everywhere. Everything seemed to run like clockwork. Some of the dormitories contained as many as fifty beds. Each one had beautifully clean sheets and was covered with a snowy white coverlet. The floors were scrubbed and polished, belying the fact that they were trodden on by dozens of little feet. The walls were plainly decorated but again clean and unmarked.

In the bedrooms there was little in the way of decoration. These were homes where money was never in great supply. God had provided only what was needed; he did not provide unnecessary frills. Each child had a special place to leave his or her clothes, which again was kept very tidy. The clothes which the children wore were a uniform. In Müller's day this was not thought strange and it was practical for every child to be wearing the same.

Müller girls wore long green and blue plaid cloaks over dresses of dull lilac cotton. Their poke bonnets were of natural coloured straw. Inside the homes they wore blue gingham pinafores over their navy and white dotted cotton dresses. Every girl had five dresses.

Inside, the girls wore their long dresses covered by a smock. These could be taken off and laundered without also having to wash the dress. The materials of Müller's day were not easy to iron.

The girls' stockings were knitted by themselves, white for summer and black for winter. Their shoes were of the ankle-strap type.

The hair-styles which the girls had were also uniform. The very young girls had their hair almost as short as the boys. This made it easy for the staff or older girls to brush it to a shiny gloss each day. From about eight to twelve they had a Dutch bob which was a short cut with a centre-parting and fringe. This was a style they could manage themselves. As the girls grew older they were allowed to grow their hair longer, where they could tie back with a ribbon or put it up.

The boys had three suits of navy blue Eton jackets, with a waistcoat over their white starched shirts plus brown corduroy trousers. In bad weather they added peak caps and short cloaks.

Indoors the boys wore white shirts, waistcoats, and long trousers. Whatever the activity in the buildings, the boys dressed in the same clothes. The small boys wore a white cotton smock, which could be easily washed and bleached.

When the five orphanages were up and running, boys, girls, and infants were all admitted. It was recorded that the youngest child ever received was only sixteen days old. The infants were too young to remember any of their life before they were at Ashley Down.

The same could not be said for the older children. They could vividly remember and were often haunted by their former life. Because of the conditions in which they had lived their early life, they were often delicate in health. The loving care they received in the homes meant that gradually they gained in physical strength and confidence. In one statement, George Müller reported, 'The low death rate in the Orphan Homes this year is of itself proof how the children are cared for physically.'

The daily timetable was strict and exacting. The children rose at six to wash and dress, the older ones helping the younger. There was then a short time of recreation when the girls knitted and the boys read. Breakfast was at eight. This was followed at half past eight by a short morning service.

At this service Müller led the children in worship and praise and commended prayers for the needs of the day. The devotions completed the girls were then assigned to bed-making. There was then a time of play for all the children inside and at ten school started.

Lessons finished at 12.30 p.m., followed by a short time playing in the playground. Dinner was just before 1.00 p.m. The boys then had a period of further school from 2.00 p.m. to 4.00 p.m. and the girls from 2.30 p.m. until 4.30 p.m. Another period of play was followed by tea just before 6.00 p.m.

For the rest of the day the children were free to play, do school preparation, or in the case of the older children do some of the jobs assigned to them. The younger children were in bed by 7.00 p.m., the older ones by 8.00 p.m.

At weekends, away from the school routines, there was time for walks, playing in the large field where the boys loved their games of football and cricket. The weekend was also the time when they were allowed large pieces of cake, often provided by the donated Harvest festivals.

Sundays were a day devoted to worship. They attended local churches in the morning, having walked to the buildings in 'crocodile' file, Bible classes in the homes in the afternoon, or evening services in the chapels.

The routine made the children feel safe when they had only known uncertainty, danger and hardship. Even by Victorian standards it was a generous and easy life. They also were able to receive discipline and Christian standards which both were invaluable to them in later life.

There were two special days each year which the children looked forward to. On Good Friday they all walked crocodile file down to the Bethesda Chapel in Great George Street. Once there they performed a singing of chosen hymns for which they had been practising for weeks. This was followed by Müller giving a special talk.

Their other exciting occasion was a day outing to Pur Down, which was a pretty spot of country within easy walking distance from Ashley Down. Each child was given a pink or blue bag of sweets to be eaten on the journey or when they were there. When they arrived, the children could play freely and enjoy a picnic which had been carried to the place in large hampers by the helpers. This was bread and cheese for lunch and bread and butter and cake for tea.

At the end of the afternoon, five balloons were released, one for each house. Looking back on these days in later years, it was always reckoned to be fine weather on the picnic days on Pur Down.

Christmas was another special time for the children. Preparations started well before the time, learning carols, practising sketches and making decorations. From the people of Bristol many, many gifts were received of dolls, chocolates, books, paint boxes, tops, marbles, and pencils. The list seemed endless, but all of the children were able to receive their own gifts.

Food was not forgotten. One Bristol wholesaler sent fruit, oranges, figs and nuts for the orphans, while another wholesaler sent flour, currants and cherries for the Christmas puddings.

But eventually the time arrived for the children to leave the homes. As each boy reached the school leaving age of fourteen, it was necessary for him to be apprenticed. They had received training in skills while they were in the homes. Many left to become clerks in the post office or to become telegraph clerks. The brighter children went on to become teachers, mostly trained at the college at Purton, Gloucester, which was financed and run by S.K.I. In theory each boy was able to choose his own form of employment.

Some of the girls went on to be trainee teachers, but most of them went into service, a job for which they were well qualified. Others went into nursing. Many returned to the homes as staff.

The boys generally left at the age of fourteen or fifteen, but girls remained at the homes until they were seventeen. Müller felt they needed protection from a wicked world for a few extra years. These ages were not rigid as Müller regarded each child as an individual.

When the time came for orphans to leave, they were provided with three outfits and they were given their travelling expenses to their employment.

Müller was always delighted to receive news of his 'old girls and boys' and later in his life he was able to meet many who had settled in other countries all round the world. Although they had had a difficult start in life, many rose to high positions in their careers.

The stories the old boys and girls were able to tell of their time in Ashley Down and their life afterwards warmed Müller's heart and the hearts of others.

William, one old boy recalled, 'My father was an alcoholic and both my parents had died by the time I was ten. I had to sleep in dustbins or under the railway arches. I did what odd jobs I could to earn money for food. Then I was discovered by a London City Missioner who sent me to Ashley Down.'

William described how his life changed. After a period of settling down, which involved fights with the other boys, he came to realise how well loved he was in the home. By the time he was old enough to leave he was apprenticed to a miller and well remembered his farewell from Müller.

Müller placed in his right hand a copy of the Bible and in his left half a crown. 'As you grip stronger with your right hand, make sure you always hang on to the Bible the tightest.'

William eventually went to New Zealand and became a preacher himself. He never forgot his time with Müller, Ashley Down and his introduction to God.

Not all the children were able to benefit from their stay in the homes. Sometimes a boy or girl was so set in his or her sinful ways that Müller had no choice but to send the child back to the relative or host family. If this happened, the child would be dismissed in front of all the children and prayed over by Müller himself.

This happened to one lad called 'Jack'. Before coming to the home he had been a liar, a thief and a mischief maker. After three years in the homes, he was still all those things. Twice he had run away taking with him belongings of the other children. The day came for him to be dismissed. Jack describes the scene himself.

'I was glad to be going. I didn't like the discipline. As Mr Müller placed his hand on my head to pray for me in front of all the other children, I refused to close my eyes and looked at his face boldly. To my amazement tears were running down that great man's face. I crumpled and cried also. At that moment I was converted and have spent the rest of my life serving God.'

9 Family matters

Mary Groves was born in 1798. As a young girl she had received a proposal of marriage from a young officer. She had felt it necessary to reject his proposal and in consequence, the young man had committed suicide. This cast a shadow on her spirit and although she had been comforted by her sister, Lydia, she still had a great sorrow.

By 1829 she was working as a companion to a sick lady, Mrs Hake, whose husband lived in Exeter. Mary's brother, Anthony Norris Groves, was working as a missionary in the East Indies and had been known slightly by Müller through the Jewish society in which they had both trained. Mary had a sweet, kind nature but also possessed an intelligent mind and had been well educated.

George met Mary at a time in his life when he was feeling it would be better to be married. Once he had got to know her, he felt she would be a suitable partner. It might have sounded a calculated way to approach marriage, but it was to prove to be a long lasting love-match.

Although Mary was attracted to George, she could not accept his proposal quickly as he could only see her when he was preaching in Exeter. But once the proposal of the 15th August 1830 had been accepted, the marriage followed on the 7th October. Fortunately, by then another companion had been found for Mrs Hake.

After the wedding, the wedding breakfast was a simple affair at the Hake's home and then after one day's honeymoon at Teignmouth, Muller went back to work the next day.

Mary was to prove an ideal partner for the austere and dour George. She was outgoing and loving, approved by all who met her; ideal attributes for the life she was to lead. Her time was spent constantly caring for the young ones, doing practical work for the homes and being a listening ear. She had started by marrying a preacher and ended up the wife of a leader of orphanages, caring for thousands of children.

In all his work, Müller was pleased by Mary, his constant companion and co-worker. He recorded in his diary that however busy he had been during the day, he would delight to spend time with her in the evening. At the end of each day Müller was happy to sit by her, holding her hand and discussing the day's affairs and the provisions of their God.

He calculated that he told her a thousand times, 'My darling, I never saw you at any time since you became my wife, without my being delighted to see you.'

In 1832, when their daughter Lydia was born, Mary was gravely ill. But God had mercy on her. She survived and although she was never as strong as previously, God still had work for her to do. She was a good mother to Lydia and a caring foster mother to the many orphans. She willingly accompanied George on his trips away or stayed patiently working at home.

Mary had a meek and kind spirit, and became the confidante of many children. It was Mary whom they could approach when her husband appeared too frightening a figure. Her husband was not the easiest of men to be married to. She nursed him when he was ill or depressed, was willing to take second place to all his many involvements and yet remained a person in her own right.

Whenever a new orphanage was opened, this caused even more work for Mrs Müller and it was due to her diligence that the opening and running of the homes was so smooth. She probably worked too hard, which undermined her general health.

Her life had been spared on more than one occasion. In 1835, she was nearly killed by a speeding carriage and in June 1838 was seriously ill and again in 1845. In the summer of 1859 she complained of weakness in her left arm

As she became older her health deteriorated. She suffered greatly from rheumatism and was often in great pain. Towards the end of 1869 she became very ill. Unsuccessfully, Müller tried to make her work less and rest more. She still worked every day at the homes, but she had to admit that she was becoming frail.

'George,' she said, 'I am becoming weaker. I do not think I will live much longer, but it is my wish to see the completion of building No. 5.'

God heard her prayer; she was spared to see the opening of the fifth building on the 6th January, 1870; but her health deteriorated fast. She caught a cold followed by a distressing cough.

'Mary, you must not walk from Lydia's home in Paul Street to Ashley Down', Müller recommended.

The doctor said the same thing: 'Mrs Müller, you are very unwell. You must rest.'

Although she rested more, she still attended to the needs of the children. On the 23rd and 30th January she was able to attend church in the mornings, but stayed at home in the evenings, to avoid the cold night air. A fire was lit in her room to bring her comfort and relief, but by the 30th she also had a severe pain across the lower part of her back and in her right arm.

On Monday she was worse and the doctor was sent for again.

'Mrs Müller has rheumatic fever. She must remain in bed.'

Mary's life was now confined to her room, her only comfort her family, her faith in God and the daily text hanging on the wall.

The text for the Tuesday, the 1st of February, from Psalm 119:75 read, 'I know, O LORD, that your judgements are right and that in faithfulness You have afflicted me.' Below that were the words of Psalm 31:15, 'My times are in Your hand.'

As Mary suffered worse pain on the Tuesday and Wednesday, she knew the words to be true.

Although George was distressed at the state of his wife's health, he tried to gain comfort from another text hanging in Mary's room; this one from Psalm 84. 'The LORD will give grace and glory, no good thing will He withhold from them that walk uprightly.'

Müller read this verse to Mary who found it helpful and repeated it regularly during the day to Lydia, who was staying with her.

On Thursday her condition worsened and on the Friday the doctor who was attending her sent for the services of another doctor. During the Saturday night she became weaker and Lydia, Mary's sister, Mrs Mannering and George stayed by her bedside.

During the afternoon of Sunday, the 6th February 1870, at twenty past four, surrounded by her family, Mary Müller died peacefully.

George and Mary had been married 39 years and 4 months. Her wish had been granted; she had lived to see the fifth orphanage opened which had been her great desire in the last few months of her life. At her funeral service, Müller extolled her virtues at great length.

George Müller was now alone, widowed and in his sixty-fifth year. How would he survive? His greatest comfort was the only surviving member of his family, Lydia.

Lydia, the only child of George and Mary Müller, was born on the 17th September 1832. In many ways hers was a lonely childhood. For the first few years of her life her mother was weak and unwell. In addition, Lydia had to share her mother with many orphans; she could not expect her mother's undivided attention. When she was only three, her baby brother had died. He had only lived for fourteen months.

Although it was the custom of the day for fathers to be distant figures, Müller was more absent than most fathers. His time was tied up with the orphans, preaching and missionary work. His little spare time in the evenings was spent with his wife.

At twelve, Lydia was sent away to boarding school. She was happy in the company of the other girls, although she studied hard and fully used her excellent mind. Undoubtedly she received a better education at the school than she would have done if she had remained at the local school.

It was while she was in boarding school that Lydia received Christ as her own personal Saviour. In a style of flowery prose, Müller was very pleased to record in his diary in April 1846, 'My beloved wife and myself had the inexpressibly great joy of receiving a letter from our beloved daughter … that she has found peace in the Lord Jesus.'

For the rest of her life, Lydia happily spent herself in the service of God. She became a respected daughter, caring for the needs of her parents. After her days of study were over, she returned home and became a companion to her mother. Much of her time was also spent in the wants of the orphaned children.

As Mary was dying, Lydia had been at her bedside and was heartbroken as she watched her mother pass into eternal life. Lydia then transferred her care to her father, but unknown to him, romance was blooming.

After Mary Müller died, George became very unwell. Ill health, both physical and emotional, had dogged him much of his life. Again the strain of losing his wife dragged his health down and he realised that he would not live for ever and the work would need to continue when he had gone.

Müller started to think about someone carrying on the work of S.K.I. The obvious choice was James Wright, who had become an invaluable help to Müller over the years.

James, who was married to his first wife at this time, felt very humbled when asked to take on this responsibility. At first he declined, as Mrs Wright was also opposed to the idea, feeling it would be too great an undertaking for her husband.

After a few weeks of prayer, and a change of heart from his wife, James Wright felt able to accept the position. It was very soon after this that Mrs Wright died and, like Müller, Wright found himself a widower.

Over the months as he worked for the orphanage, Wright often met Lydia who was caring for her father as well as working for the orphans. As two lonely people, they continued to meet during their work and a love grew between them. They had the same ideals in life, loving and serving God, as well as loving and caring for the welfare of the orphans.

In August 1871 Wright approached Müller, saying, 'I have come to ask the hand of your daughter, Lydia, in marriage.'

Müller was amazed. He'd been so wrapped in his own work and his grief that he had no idea that romance was in the air.

To Wright's relief, Müller replied, 'I know of no one to whom I would so willingly entrust this my choicest earthly treasure.'

Lydia's only hesitation in accepting this offer of marriage was that she would be relinquishing the care of her father. Müller proved to her that it was also his will that she should be married to James Wright and so when Lydia Müller was thirty-nine years of age, she was married to James Wright on the 16th of November, 1871. James was to be very blessed to have two marriages, which would both last for eighteen years.

But romance was still in the air.

This left George alone and lonely himself. He needed a companion and soul mate. In the church was a highly regarded spinster lady, Miss Susannah Grace Sangar, twenty years his junior, whom he had known for twenty-five years. Susannah was a governess to a family by the name of Armstrong in Clifton.

To marry again was a matter which received a great amount of prayer. There was no way he could replace Mary, but he was not willing to spend his days alone. Müller recorded in his diary, 'I have every reason to believe that she would prove a great helper to me in my various services.' Not a very romantic approach, but certainly a practical one.

The news of the marriage stunned the church when it was suddenly announced at a Friday evening meeting. They had never considered the thought that Müller might marry again. Nevertheless, on the 30th November, 1871, only two weeks after the marriage of Lydia and James, Müller was married to Susannah.

Susannah was to prove to be a very different lady from Mary, but Müller came to realise that in each of his marriages he had the right wife at the right time.

9 Extending horizons

Susannah Sangar was in her late forties when she married Müller. He spoke of her with affection and respect, in his narrative calling her 'my dear wife'. But in many ways Susannah was a very different lady from Mary. Her interest in the care of the orphans was not so great and she was not willing to sit at home daily caring for their needs. In many ways the compatibility of George with his second wife was less fulfilling.

However, during the first two years of their marriage Susannah proved to be a help in the office of the homes. Her organisational skills were useful as she helped to deal with much of the correspondence. Then in March 1874 she became desperately ill.

Susannah was staying with Lydia on Thursday, the 16th of March, when Lydia sent an urgent message to Müller at Ashley Down: 'Susannah is haemorrhaging.'

George knew that his wife was ill, but hadn't realised how serious it was. By the time Müller had rushed to his wife's bedside, the doctor was already in attendance. He announced to the stunned George, 'Mr Müller, your wife has typhoid fever.'

As Susannah hovered between life and death, many thousands of prayers were offered up all over the world. Spring turned into summer and Susannah slowly recovered, but not to full health. Her mind had become very disturbed through her illness and she became used to the attention that had been heaped upon her.

In her convalescence she demanded a few changes. No longer did she wish to live in Paul Street. It was Susannah who persuaded Müller also to set up a home in No. 3. When she was there she could be near the centre of all the activity. At the home she had a special garden laid out for her, which she found a great comfort.

Susannah also had itchy feet and wanted to travel. Providently this idea fell in with George's own ideas. Müller knew the time had come for him to re-assess his life. At the age of seventy he needed to talk to God about what he should be doing for the remainder of his life.

The work of the five homes was up and running. The staff and workers were very capable. James Wright, with Lydia by his side, was proving to be an excellent leader. After prayer, Müller realised that he was approaching the time of life when he could be what in his youth he had longed to be—a travelling missionary and evangelist.

Gradually he realised it was God's leading, with Susannah by his side, to tour the world telling of the work and preaching the Word. He knew he wasn't the most talented preacher, but he did know he had a story to tell and a gospel to spread.

The plan was that each year the Müllers would go on tour and then in the summer period, for about a month, they would take over the running of S.K.I. and the orphanages while the Wrights had a rest. During this time, Müller would write his annual report.

One of the reasons for Müller desiring to travel and preach at this time was in the interest of church unity. He recorded in his diary, 'I wish to break down the barriers of denominationalism and spread brotherly love amongst true Christians. Though not agreeing with some opinions and practices, I will nevertheless preach amongst all, having seen for many years how greatly the heart of Lord Jesus must be grieved by the disunion that exists among his own true disciples.'

Müller still bore a great sadness for the lack of harmony which had been displayed within the Brethren movement. He wished to follow his master's example and love all Christians.

Müller was often asked who paid for all their trips and he recorded that all the expenses were met by donors who had felt the need from God to give. George continued the practice that he had used for so many years of never asking for money.

Susannah would prove to be an excellent companion in his proposed travels. Although she never stood on the platform herself, she made sure that George worked hard and played hard during their trips. She supported him emotionally and was by his side to nurse him and help him on the many occasions when he felt exhausted or ill.

Susannah dealt faithfully with Müller's correspondence, proving herself to be an excellent secretary-*cum*-nurse-*cum*-companion. Wherever they were to travel in the world, she never seemed to mind the heat or cold, the deprivations or the tiredness.

As time went by, Susannah proved herself to be a writer, writing a book about the life of George Müller and one a personal account of their travels. Entitled *A Brief Account of the life and Labours of George Müller,* and *The Preaching Tours and Missionary Labours of George Müller,* these books were soon selling at one shilling and three shillings and sixpence respectively. Whereas Müller always wrote kindly and lovingly, Susannah sometimes displayed a caustic style, condemning of some of the strange practices which they witnessed on their travels.

Their first tour was by way of an experiment. On the 26th March, 1875, they travelled to Brighton and then on to London. Müller was able to preach three times at the Mildmay Conference held in the city. In his meticulous way, George recorded that there were 3,000 hearers at each of the meetings. Then through the invitation of Charles Haddon Spurgeon, one of the most popular evangelists of the day, Müller was able to preach at the Metropolitan Tabernacle. The lives of Müller and Spurgeon were to cross on various occasions and they had a mutual respect for each other.

While in the capital Müller's preaching extended to the 'Edinburgh Castle' in the East End of London. This was a public house commandeered as a 'centre of evangelism' by Dr Thomas Barnardo.

Thomas Barnardo and George Müller also had a great deal in common, having both established children's homes. Although their time together was brief, they compared notes, discussed strategies and above all gave the glory to God for his love and provision.

The Müllers continued north to Sunderland and Newcastle before returning to Bristol on the 6th July. The *Narrative* records that he preached seventy times on this tour.

Back in Bristol in August, Dr Dwight Moody, from the United States was able to meet Müller. Along with Ira Sankey he had been conducting evangelistic campaigns in England and he had once described Müller as one of the three people whom he would most like to meet in this country. In the environment of Ashley Down, they had much they were able to discuss, not least to praise and glorify God.

On their return Müller found the homes running very smoothly. James and Lydia were continuing the orphanages in the same manner that Müller had commenced them. His mind free from anxiety on that score, soon he was planning his next trip.

Their next journey was to include Scotland and Ireland and to continue the work that Moody and Sankey had started in England. In the middle of August 1875, they travelled north, stopping to preach in Liverpool for five weeks. Here in the Victoria Hall, which had been built for the Moody and Sankey missions, they had probably their largest audiences.

It was not all about numbers, it was about people. Every time Müller preached, people repented and were converted from their old ways. One of Müller's old boys, the commander of a large merchant vessel docked in Liverpool, attended the first of Müller's meeting in the city. He heard the message and for the first time was convicted of his sins and was converted.

'Mr Müller,' he managed to speak to the great man after the service, 'I spent many years under your care at Bristol and although I heard the gospel, I never thought it applied to me. But tonight, I realised that I was a sinner and needed to repent.'

Müller smiled. This was the purpose of his work; this was the reason for his tours.

In Scotland, Susannah records that while staying in the village of Crathie, they were shown over Balmoral Castle by a Christian housekeeper. A short time before they left the village Queen Victoria herself arrived for a visit and they were able to see her driving out occasionally. Susannah especially enjoyed her brushes with royalty. Müller was more interested in the fact that he counted the King of kings as his friend.

The Müllers arrived back from their northern tour in July 1876, but the next month they were off again. This time they visited Switzerland, Germany and Holland. It was a trip full of memories for Müller.

In Germany, he remembered his childhood—his mother, father and brother. Only too easily he brought to mind his stealing, cheating, drinking and thoroughly debased character. The visit to his first Bible meeting with Beta was still vivid in his mind. It seemed hard to believe that fifty years on he was the same person. Indeed, he wasn't the same person; he had been changed, protected and used by God. He rejoiced greatly.

For most of the tour Müller preached in English or German. He was happy to be able to use his native tongue again. Sometimes he even spoke in halting French. When none of these languages were understood, he had an interpreter.

Susannah also made sure there was time for sight-seeing and a period of relaxation for her husband. They crossed Lake Lucerne on a steamer and ascended the Rigi in the Alps by cog-wheel railway for views across the Bernese Oberland and the Black Forest. Müller remembered when he had first been in Switzerland and climbed the Rigi with his school friend, Beta. He also recalled with shame how he'd cheated his friends out of some of the travelling expenses. How kindly God had dealt with him since that time.

Susannah made sure they went through the St Gothard Pass, which was shrouded in mist, but they could still marvel at the beauty of the place, as the creation of God's hand was everywhere.

At Stuttgart they had another brush with royalty. The Queen of Wurttemberg interviewed Müller about his work in Bristol. Also Princess Karl, mother-in-law of Princess Alice of England, Princess von Battenberg and several other royal personages meet with the Müller at Darmstadt.

Then the couple returned to England, Müller to write his next narrative, Susannah to recount their adventures. Plans were made for their next tour. This was led by Susannah's driving ambition, but George was only too willing to preach and share the Word of God with as many people and as far round the world as possible.

Müller had received many pressing invitations to preach in North America. On their return to England more such invitations were waiting for them. Therefore for a whole year during 1877 and 1878 the Müllers toured Canada and the United States.

The journey across the Atlantic was not without an opportunity to witness. A thick fog lay across the water which was delaying the journey. Müller was worried he was going to be late for his first appointment. He spoke to the captain, saying, 'I have never been late for an appointment yet. Let's pray that God will clear the fog.'

The captain was sceptical. Müller prayed nevertheless. Then he said, 'I know God has answered my prayers. Look outside; you will see the fog has gone.'

The captain looked. The fog had gone. After that day the captain was continually repeating the story and asserting that was the day he began to believe in God. God could use even the fog to convict a man of the state of his soul.

George's reputation went before him. He was now known as a world-wide evangelist. After being overwhelmed by the majesty of the Niagara Falls, Müller and Susannah were able to visit many important American cities; sometimes the audience was white, sometimes black. George wanted his message to be for all.

It was a tour of extreme temperatures. At Sherman, in St Louis, which at 8,235 feet above sea-level, they suffered intense cold, the railway station being the then highest in the world. At Stockton, in the southern states, the heat was tremendous.

Susannah recorded in her diary, 'We had a tremendous conflict with mosquitoes, but although we killed them by the score, could do very little in the way of exterminating the foe.'

Before returning home the couple received an invitation to the White House, where Müller was in audience with President Hayes for half an hour. As well as discussing the work for the children, Müller also talked about the state of the president's soul.

The list of places where the Müllers visited and George preached would shame any travel itinerary today—Washington, Salem in Virginia, Columbia in South Carolina, Jacksonville, New Orleans, St Louis, San Francisco.

While touring the United States, it was a tremendous joy for Müller to meet up with 'old boys and girls'. They remembered with affection their time in the homes in Bristol and mostly they were doing very well in the 'new country'. He was even more delighted when he learned that they had absorbed the truths they had learned in their childhood and were following God.

His greatest joy was to meet with old boys or girls who had left their homeland and were doing well. Müller often had the joy of meeting the next generation, his 'grandchildren'.

'Sir, I remember you at Bristol. When I left the homes I married a kind Christian gentleman and now we have two children who we are bringing up to honour the Lord.'

'Mr Müller, I was one of your boys at Ashley Down. I want you to know sir that I now have a good job in this country and I continue to love God.'

Such encounters thrilled Müller's heart. He was able to see the harvest which he and others had sown.

Meeting at Mentone and other travels

For their fifth tour, which was to last ten months, George and Susannah went east to southern Europe. For the first time Müller was able to visit schools in Spain, which for the last ten years had been supported by the Scriptural Knowledge Institution.

At one of the schools in Barcelona Müller was able to tell the 150 pupils about the children in Ashley Down. The Spanish children knew what it was to be bereft of parents and to receive love and care from Christian people. Although an interpreter had to be used, the children were still able to appreciate the passion with which Müller spoke about the work and his love for the Lord.

In Mentone, France, Charles Spurgeon was already staying there when Müller visited. Spurgeon was in the habit of finding rest and healing at Mentone and was delighted also to receive as guests the Rev J. Hudson Taylor, founder of the China Inland Mission and Pastor John Bost founder and conductor of the asylum of La Force, in France.

The four men enjoyed their time together discussing the various aspects of their work. Müller and Spurgeon recalled the time when they had previously met at the Metropolitan Tabernacle in London four years earlier and how God had led them both since that time.

Spurgeon wrote an account of the meeting in his May magazine, which he entitled 'Interviews with three of the King's Captains'. He said of his meeting with Müller, 'The simple, childlike, holy trust of Müller was overpowering. He is not a sanctimonious person, but full of real joy.'

Hudson Taylor, the best known of the missionaries to China at that time, had special reason to be grateful to Müller. For many years he was one of the missionaries supported by S.K.I. One spring Taylor had been robbed in Ningpo. Müller had sent £40 to help with the loss. A few years later Taylor found it necessary to resign from the Chinese Evangelical Society. At that time in 1863, Müller again sent him money: this time £10.

After Taylor had formed the China Inland Mission, the Yangchow riots occurred and Müller increased his giving. Libel stories circulated and giving to Taylor decreased. Although Müller did not realise this at the time, he still had faith in the missionary, and again increased his giving. Taylor's losses were soon made up by the extra giving.

This all happened at a time when Müller had 187 other missionaries he was supporting. Müller often recalled a quote from Hudson Taylor, 'Satan may build a barrier about us, but he can never roof us in, so that we cannot look up.'

The part of the tour spent in Italy, included viewing the sights as well as preaching—climbing Vesuvius, a trip in a Venetian gondola, sight-seeing in Rome, Florence and San Remo.

Once Müller had started on his tours, his pattern of life changed completely. During the few summer months when they were in England, he would attend to any outstanding business connected with the orphanages. Then as the autumn approached, the next tour would commence.

After spending ten weeks back in Bristol, on the 7th August, 1879, George and Susannah set off for the United States to honour the many invitations Müller had received to visit there. At one church Susannah was amused by the introduction that was given her husband, 'My dear friends, I rejoice to tell you that we are about to hear the gospel from the heart and lips of our venerable friend, who, though now aged seventy-four, has preached the gospel upwards of one thousand four hundred times in the last four years, in the various cities and countries he has visited.'

At one city he found he was preaching to German immigrants. His heart went out to them. He could still remember his feelings at leaving his homeland and living in a strange city where the people spoke in an unfamiliar tongue. He wanted the immigrants to know that they had a friend who could never let them down.

In 1880 George and Susannah found it necessary to return to Canada and the United States. Again Müller was able to preach to displaced Germans. They found there were thousands of immigrants pouring in from Germany and Switzerland and were amazed to learn that there were nine million Germans in the country at that time.

Later in the tour, Müller was particularly pleased to visit Yale University, as he recalled, 'I was converted myself while a student at the University of Halle.'

In New York the couple experienced the coldest winter that had been known in the city for thirty years. The ferry ships had difficulty cutting their way through the ice on the river.

The next year, 1881, saw the couple again on their travels, this time to Egypt, Palestine, Turkey and Greece. It was the type of tour that would have defeated people half their age. By this time George was seventy-six and Susannah in her late fifties.

This next tour, their eighth, was noted for its hardships. The ship on which they were sailing was not able to land at Jaffa because of rough seas, so they had to board a small boat, rowed by eight Arabs through very high waves. The road journey from Jaffa to Jerusalem was described by Müller as, 'worse than the worst roads in Europe'.

They felt very pleased to be able to travel round the Holy Land, seeing the sights which Jesus would have seen—Jerusalem, the Mount of Olives, Brook Kidron and the reputed old house of Lazarus; so many of the biblical stories came to life through their visit. In the future, when they read of these places in the Bible, they would recall their visit to them.

In connection with biblical prediction, Susannah noted, 'There is no indication whatever of any gathering of Jews on an extensive scale from other countries to their own land.'

Fortunately, Susannah was not to know of the intensely disturbing historical events which would befall the country from the time of their visit to the present day.

Their time at Haifa among the German settlers brought about a revival. To have a preacher from their homeland was very special to them. As well as preaching, the couple had time to visit the Pyramids, Cairo and Alexandria.

May 1882 saw the Müllers back at Ashley Down. There had been concern expressed that with Müller absent for such long periods, the level of donations would fall. To Müller's joy, this did not prove to be the case. This showed to Müller and others that the work was not of Müller, but of God. It was to his glory and he would provide for it.

The couple were back in England, but not for long; they seemed to have unlimited strength. In August of that year, they were again off on their tours.

This time they went to Germany, Austria, Hungary, Bohemia, Russia and Poland and even up to Lapland. Müller was able to show to Susannah the city of Halberstaedt where he had gone to school and the cathedral where he had taken his first communion. He also showed her his father's house which was still standing in the town of Kroppenstadt.

He received a warm welcome to preach in these places, as he was a 'local boy made good' and in Halle was able to meet up with two men who had been students with him over sixty years before.

But, apart from the happy times spent in his former homeland, the lasting memory of this tour was the lack of religious freedom, particularly in Austria and Russia. In spite of this while they were in Russia, they were able to stay for eleven weeks in the vast house belonging to a Colonel Paschoff and Princess Lieven, who had both been converted a few years earlier.

Müller had to be very careful where he preached without a permit. Not knowing what the limits were, he preached to twenty in Paschoff's house. Before long he was summoned to appear before the Director of Police, as he had gone beyond his permit. Müller did not wish to be imprisoned on German soil again. He still had memories of his youthful imprisonment. This meant he was no longer able to preach at the Colonel's house.

The Evangelical Movement in Russia was being suppressed. Many Christians had been banished from their estates, exiled from the country or even sent to Siberia. Although the Tsar was sympathetic to the beliefs, he was too weak to make a stand. Müller would not be alive to see the Revolution of 1917, but it would not have surprised him.

Aged travellers

S ince Müller was first converted in his twenties, he had always felt a leaning to be a missionary in India. Four times he had offered himself, but God had other ideas, and it was not to be. However, in September 1883, at the age of seventy-eight, he again had the call to go to India. This time it would be as an old man accompanied by his wife, not a young missionary with little experience of life.

George and Susannah were able to engage an Indian servant, Abraham, to accompany them on their travels. They found the servant, who was able to speak Hindustani, Tamil and Canarese, a great help to them and they became very attached to him. They were able to travel 21,000 miles around the vast continent and Müller preached 206 times. As a seasoned traveller, he was still able to wonder at the marvels of God's creation. In Darjeeling he recorded, 'The grandeur and magnificence of the highest mountain in the world, perpetually covered in snow will never be erased from any God-fearing person who has seen it.'

Susannah felt very emotional when standing at the site of the Indian mutiny and regretted that the British Government still didn't allow Christian teaching in the Lahore prison and the areas of idolatry at Benares. She was so moved that she wrote to Christians back home urging them to leave the comforts of England and offer themselves as missionaries.

A very tired couple returned to Bristol and because of their advancing age and the rigours of life style, both George and Susannah had a period of ill health. While touring England and South Wales, Susannah had an attack of erysipelas, a streptococcal infection which turned her face and scalp a deep red colour. The doctor advised returning to Bristol immediately.

The next tour, which was meant to be in England and Ireland, was cut short because George had a violent cold while still in Shropshire and therefore they were not able to continue to Ireland. Instead, they rested in the Isle of Wight. And in September 1885 they only ventured as far as

Liverpool and Dundee. But theirs was only a short period of ill health and before long they had returned to full health and continued on their worldwide tours.

Their next trip, which included countries they had not previously visited, commenced in November 1885 and ended in June 1887. Müller began by three weeks of engagements in New York. The couple then crossed the continent by train and set sail from San Francisco for Australia. George preached in the major cities, Sydney, Melbourne and Brisbane where they sailed for Java.

Because no interpreter could be found in that place, they moved on to Hong Kong and Shanghai. While Müller was in China, he was again able to meet Hudson Taylor and many of the missionaries working with him. For many years Müller had been financially and prayerfully supporting the work of the China Inland Mission.

George and Susannah then sailed for Japan, arriving at Nagasaki and moving on to preach at Yokohama, Tokyo, Kobe, Kioto and Osaka. In these cities he had to have the use of an interpreter.

Not surprisingly when they returned to Hong Kong, George was again laid low with a severe cold. Nevertheless, it seemed impossible that a man of his age could cope with such a punishing itinerary. Before returning home they visited and George preached in Singapore, Penang and Colombo. Travelling back through Europe they passed through Marseilles and Nice. On their round-the-world trip they had travelled 37,280 miles.

After only two months they were off again on their next tour, lasting from August 1887 to March 1890. On this visit to Australia, they started on the west coast—Albany, Adelaide and fifteen other towns. It was a gruelling programme with Müller preaching up to six or seven times each week. From Melbourne they sailed to Tasmania and then on to New Zealand.

Keeping up the same frantic pace they returned to Australia, this time to Sydney, then on to Ceylon and to the continent of India.

While in Calcutta in December, Müller continued with his punishing programme despite the intense heat and continual menace of mosquitoes. Even at night there was no relief from either. Müller became very unwell and Susannah became alarmed for his health. She called a doctor. The servant, John Nathaniel, they had hired, was able to interpret.

'The doctor says unless you leave Calcutta immediately, your husband's life will be at risk. He advises you to catch a train to Darjeeling.'

On the journey to Darjeeling, George was so overcome by the heat that Susannah thought he was going to die right there on the train. She persuaded him to lie down on the floor while she opened all the windows to catch every breath of air. All night she continued to fan him with a large fan they had with them and persuaded him to drink a little wine or water.

John Nathaniel was urged to get a cup of tea or even a glass of lemonade at each station where the train stopped. Susannah prayed that God would not let him die in a place so far away from home. By Susannah's care, John Nathaniel's drinks and God's providence, George Müller was kept alive during the night and the next day. When they arrived at Damookdea Ghat, they were quickly able to board the ferry-steamer and the refreshing breezes on the lake quickly revived him.

'I am so thankful that through the Lord's kindness, Mr Müller was soon fit and well again,' Susannah recorded.

Although she was not always an 'easy' person, her care and attention undoubtedly kept alive this man who had been so delicate in his youth. Müller was now eighty-four and able to travel the world, executing an extremely busy programme. Physically as well as spiritually he was not the same man he had been in his youth.

While in Jubbulpore they received a telegram with devastating news.

'Regret to inform you of the death of my wife, Lydia, signed James Wright.'

Müller was heartbroken. His only surviving relative had died. He had lost a son, a wife and now a daughter. He had not expected Lydia to pre-decease him. It was Lydia who had been at his side when Mary had died and comforted him in his months of loneliness. Now she was gone.

After thirty years of working at the orphan homes, at the age of fifty-eight, Lydia had died on the 10th of January, 1890. Müller had very nearly lost his own life in India; now he had to face the grief of losing his beloved daughter. He had no idea that Lydia had been ill and her death was a great blow to him. He felt that his last link with Mary, his first wife, had now been severed. In Müller's eyes, fifty-eight was far too young to die.

Mr and Mrs Müller's plans were immediately changed. They needed to return to England as soon as possible. Although Müller still found opportunity to preach on their return journey, the sad couple were soon back in Bristol. George confessed to being 'in much need of rest'.

But the rest didn't last for long. In August 1890 they travelled to Germany and Switzerland, staying for a total of a year and nine months. After suffering from the extreme heat in India, they now had to endure intense cold during the winter months. Every city they visited, Müller preached. He even preached at Halberstadt, Heimersleben and Magdeburg, not as the gangling youth of his former days, but as an aging preacher of worldwide renown.

In his report Müller described some of the discomforts they had encountered during their various travels. 'During some tours we have been exposed to cold from fifty to fifty-six degrees below freezing. At other times heat of one hundred and ten degrees and upwards.'

In Calcutta, where they had worked for fifteen weeks, the temperature had been 115 degrees in the shade and they had had to retreat to the cooler Himalayas.

Travelling by land had often been hazardous. Some journeys had been of twenty or thirty hours' duration. Some train journeys had lasted six days and nights.

The animal kingdom had often been a nuisance. They had been 'exceedingly tried by insects'. In the United States, New South Wales, Ceylon and in India the mosquitoes had been 'most grievous'. On two first-class steamers, rats had overrun them at night.

The sea trips had caused other hazards. Gales and typhoons had been experienced. Occasionally they feared for their lives and had prayed earnestly for deliverance.

The Lord had constantly provided money for these tours and Müller was always prepared to pay fares and hotel bills from the money he had been given. It was not his practice to look for hospitality from the Christian people he met on his travels. When this did happen, Müller recorded it carefully in his reports.

'I thank the Lord for the hospitality we have received.'

In his narrative, he also records, 'In the twelve years from 1874 to 1885 we received £30,000 in gifts for personal use, of which more than £27,000 has been given away. I have also spent many hundreds out of my own means.'

Of his travels, Müller was able to record: 'Hitherto has the Lord helped us and no doubt will help us to the end.'

For Susannah Müller, the end was very near.

Last days

George and Susannah returned from their last tour in May 1892. It was time to take stock. He made a careful review of all the work being done. In July he prayerfully came to the conclusion that there should be no more expansion of the children's work. He had been planning to build two more houses, but this would have meant getting into debt. Müller was not prepared to do this.

Some of the Day Schools were closed down, with the exception of the Spanish, Italian and the three United Kingdom ones. The training of teachers at Purton would continue, as would the Sunday Schools.

The Ashley Down site covered nineteen acres. In 1893 Müller sold ten acres on which he had planned to build the two further houses. Great men like Shaftesbury and Dickens had highlighted the needs of the poor. In addition other children's homes had been established—Fegan's, Barnardo's, the Church of England. The social problems at the end of the nineteenth century were not as great as they had been sixty years earlier.

There was also to be great change in Müller's personal life. Susannah fell ill. After an illness of many months, with Müller often in attendance at his wife's bedside, Susannah died on the 13th of January, 1894. George was full of thankfulness for his twenty-three years and six months of marriage to her. With his two marriages, he had had a total of 'sixty–two years of married life'.

At the time Müller was able to quote from Psalm 34: 'I will bless the LORD at all times; His praise shall continually be in my mouth.'

Reviewing his marriages, Müller was able to see the hand of God at work. He realised that as he became older, Mary would not have been able to cope with the rigours of the travelling. Mary was the wife he needed in his younger days when he was setting up the orphanages in Bristol. Susannah was the wife he needed when he was touring the world.

But now Müller was left without a wife or daughter. He did not dwell on his sadness; instead he was able to rejoice in it. He knew the three females in his life were now at peace; they had no more earthly sufferings.

Müller still owned the house at No. 21 Paul Street, but he was now left on his own, so he decided to sell it. Paul Street was a road that would not survive the expansion of Bristol; today most of the houses have been pulled down and replaced by lock-up garages. Müller now had a suite of rooms in orphanage No. 3 as well as his study which he had used there for many years. No. 3 was to be his home for the rest of his life.

His study was small and Spartan in content. There was a table, a chair, one or two ordinary chairs for visitors, and a single armchair. The desk was flat-topped with several drawers—an ordinary, typical desk for the period, but with what memories imprinted into the very woodwork! What prayers uttered and tears shed over it!

The room would have witnessed many distraught grandparents making arrangements to leave orphaned children; other orphans would have met Müller before they went out into the world, receiving a blessing and final words of advice from Müller. In this room Mary and George would often have met for their precious time together, when Müller recorded how pleased he always was to see his wife.

This was now the period of his life when Müller would be visited, instead of doing the visiting himself. The Earl of Derby, Lord Salisbury and Lord Hampton were among those who came to Ashley Down at some time.

Charles Dickens visited partly because he had heard a rumour that the children were badly treated and often hungry. Critics of good works always did abound. When confronted by Dickens, Müller handed the bunch of keys for the five houses to an assistant, saying, 'Take Mr Dickens round and show him whatever he wants to see.'

Dickens left eventually well satisfied and admiring of all that he had seen.

Even in old age Müller had a striking appearance. Six feet tall, or *high* as Müller would have said, still quite upright, with locks of silver hair, his face bore the distinctive outlines of a refined German of military bearing. A farmer had once described him as having 'the twenty-third Psalm written all over his face'.

George Müller's birthday had always been the excuse for a celebration for the children at Ashley Down. Fortunately the 27th of September coincided with the blackberry season. Collected berries with locally grown apples made delicious pies.

His ninetieth birthday was an occasion to be remembered. The people at the Bethesda Chapel gave him a special presentation of a writing table with a flexible cover and also a purse with £150–£200. Because of Müller's advancing years it was not a table that ever had a great deal of use. The congregation noted that his voice seemed as strong as ever; his movements were quick and he appeared not to suffer from rheumatism.

Müller wrote in his diary, 'My mind is still as clear as it was when I passed my university examinations.'

The people of Bristol had not known him as a young man when he had always been suffering from one illness or another. His ailments then had been caused by his previous reckless lifestyle. Since God had taken first place in his life, his health had improved.

At the ceremony, a Christian gentleman said to him, 'When you die and go to heaven, it will be like a ship sailing into harbour under full sail.'

George wisely replied, 'No, it will be poor George Müller who has to pray each day, "Hold me up, Lord, that my footsteps may not slip."'

Müller was asked to share what he considered had been the power behind his ministry. George answered dramatically, 'There was a day when I died, utterly died.'

His amazed questioner waited for the explanation.

'I died to George Müller,' he continued, 'I died to his opinions, his will, his preferences. Since then I have studied only to show myself approved to God.'

For well over sixty years that simple statement had been the secret of Müller's life. He knew he'd made mistakes and sometimes made enemies, but his whole life had been spent trying to please God.

He had often prayed, 'Oh Lord, may my last days be my best.'

His God had not disappointed him. He refused to carry a stick and tried to maintain his upright posture, which for so many years had been his trademark. He still gave out the notices from the pulpit, although his listeners could sometimes count at least three mistakes. He had reached an age when he no longer preached.

George lived for another four years after the death of Susannah. In his last years although he did not preach he still wrote his annual report. He continued his missionary involvement and received visitors. To one visitor he confessed, 'Every day I pray for the two sons of a friend of my youth. They are not converted yet, but they will be. George Müller never gives up.'

Many years earlier he had confessed that he was praying for the conversion of five particular people. One was converted after eighteen months, a second after five years and another after six years. The fourth person turned to God just before Müller died and the last a few years after his death. Müller never gave up.

The 20th of June, 1897, was Jubilee Sunday. Queen Victoria was celebrating her Diamond Jubilee. Hers was the longest reign of a British monarch so far. It was three years before Victoria came to the throne that Müller had started the Scriptural Knowledge Institution. He was caring for children in Wilson Street before her reign commenced.

Müller broke his self-imposed rule by preaching the sermon on that Jubilee Sunday. How eagerly his words were received! What knowledge he had to impart! They were listening to a man who had once confessed in a letter to the British and Foreign Bible Society that he had read the Bible over a thousand times.

The congregation knew he couldn't live for ever and they didn't wish to miss a single word of what he had to say. He did not seem to be weakening, but there was no getting round the fact that he was well over ninety.

To mark the Jubilee, Müller also arranged for all the children to visit Bristol Zoo. It was a rare treat which many remembered for years afterwards.

During the summer of 1897 he was persuaded to have a week's rest at Bishopsteignton in Devon.

'I must be busy while I am there,' Müller commented. 'Can it be arranged for me to preach while I am staying there?'

It was soon arranged for him to preach in both Bishopsteignton and Teignmouth. Müller could clearly remember when he had first preached in that area and had met his beloved Mary. What adventures he had had since that time and how wonderfully he had been kept by God.

Back in Bristol he began to preach occasionally, though he found the winter cold hard to endure. His last sermon was on the morning of the 6th March 1898 at Clifton in the Alma Road Chapel. He spoke from Isaiah 6, comparing it with John 12:37–41. It was a powerful sermon, though none could know it would be his last.

Müller worked as usual at his desk on the Monday, Tuesday and Wednesday following. He also received visitors and was able to rejoice with them that he could still be used by God in active service. One friend brought greetings from Robert C. Chapman, the man who had been responsible for bringing Craik and Müller to Bristol. Chapman and Müller had enjoyed a friendship of sixty-eight years.

On Wednesday he confessed to James Wright that he had felt faint while dressing that morning. Three times had had to stop and rest.

'Do you think you should have an attendant in your room?' asked James.

Later in the day Müller declared that he was feeling better but promised he would have an attendant the following night.

Meanwhile he had the evening prayers to take at No. 3. When he retired that night he seemed as usual.

He was certainly all right when he met a pupil teacher on the stairs. George stood quietly at the top of the flight. With the impatience of youth, the young lady was running up the stairs two steps at a time singing, 'I know not what awaits me, God kindly veils my eyes.'

Müller, ever the gentleman, shook hands with her as she passed, saying, 'I'm so glad you're happy, but you must not run up the stairs two at a time. You might hurt yourself.'

The pupil teacher was the last person to see George Müller alive. During the night at about five or six o'clock, he got out of bed and reached for a glass of milk and biscuit, which were always on his dressing table at night. Again he had a fainting fit and as he fell he clutched at the cloth, scattering the items over the carpet.

The next morning when the maid entered the room, she found him on the floor. During the night of the 10th March 1898, the great George Müller had died and entered into his reward.

As he lay on his bedroom floor, his nephew, Edward Kennaway Groves, who had been visiting the orphanages at that time, kissed him. Edward's testimony was that Müller had 'never told him a lie'. What a contrast from

Müller's youth, when he had prided himself on his ability to lie and be believed.

Although Müller was ninety-two, the news came as a shock to the people of Bristol. His death hadn't been preceded by noticeably failing health. For many people George Müller and his homes on Ashley Down had always been there.

On the Sunday after his death every church in the city made reference to it. In true Victorian vein, some even played the *Dead March* during the service. Many of the people who had prayed on Sunday attended his funeral on Monday, the 14th.

By his special request, the funeral was a simple affair with no flowers, but it was impossible to stop the Bristol townsfolk making it into a special occasion. All the shutters were up in the main street. Flags were at half-mast on the Bristol Cathedral and other churches. Muffled bells sounded throughout the entire city. Tens of thousands lined the funeral route. Müller had been a noted citizen of Bristol for sixty-five years.

Most memorable of all was the behaviour of the orphans themselves. According to James Wright they had cried copiously when they heard of Müller's death. On the funeral day they were still crying. Especially saddened was the poor pupil teacher who had been the last to see him alive. The older orphans were allowed to walk along the route behind the coffin.

A photo taken of the funeral procession in George Street as it entered Park Street, showed at least thirty-five carriages following the cortege. The police controlled the watching crowds well, though at the quieter ceremony at Arno's Vale, without the police presence, pickpockets had a field day.

The simple funeral service was divided into two parts: the first at the Bethesda church and the second at the Arno's Vale Cemetery. Because of the number of the mourners, it took an hour to reach the cemetery. Once there, George Müller was buried beside his two wives.

The headstone, which was put up later, was paid for by past and present orphans. In fact, so great was the receipt of donations that James Wright had to stop the flow of money. There were so many men and women worldwide who were indebted to Müller for the foundation of their faith.

The amount of money Müller left when he died was only £150. When one American newspaper reported the fact, three noughts were added to make the figure more respectable. How little they understood Müller's secret or life. His wealth had not been in money; it had been invested in his God.

For the press it was a marvellous opportunity to have a different source of news. The *Times* and *Daily Telegraph* both included obituaries. Different papers reported the story of his life in different ways. Many, like the *Western Daily Press*, treated him as a philanthropist and completely omitted to mention his driving force—God. The *Liverpool Mercury* was an exception. After mentioning his achievements, it said, 'How was this wonder accomplished? Mr Müller has told the world that it was the result of Prayer. The rationalism of the day will sneer at this declaration, but the facts remain to be explained.'

The *Daily Telegraph* accurately recorded, 'Mr Müller's life and example, by their eloquent and touching beauty, cannot fail to impress even a sceptical and utilitarian age.'

They also added in a flash of flowery journalism, 'He had robbed the cruel streets of thousands of victim, the gaols of thousands of felons, the workhouse of thousands of helpless waifs.'

The *Bristol Times*, which was the voice of citizens who knew him best, said, 'It may be taken as substantiated that nearly all which has been said about Mr Müller is absolutely true.'

And another quote from the same paper would have caused a quiet nod and wry smile from the great man; 'He was raised up for the purpose of showing that the age of miracles is not past.'

Müller once recorded in his diary, 'There has never been a single day that I failed to get an audience with the King.'

And his final message, 'My faith is the same faith which is found in every believer. Try it for yourself.'

But not the end—the work carries on

BY JULIAN MARSH, CHIEF EXECUTIVE, THE GEORGE MÜLLER FOUNDATION

From the first orphanage in Wilson Street opened by Müller on the 11th April 1836, through the imposing and magnificent orphanages at Ashley Down, to the smaller family-based residential children's homes (called family group homes) which had all closed by the mid-80s, to the Day Care, Community and Family Care work from the mid-80s to 2003, and to the work of today which is to help local churches to become more effective in faith, care and evangelism amongst children, families and young people (especially the most needy), Müllers has continued to serve God. The needs that Müllers has been addressing have varied over the years. Society's needs are very different today compared with what they were in the 1830s. Today, children in need of care or who are orphaned are only a comparatively small number in the UK. However, throughout each generation, there has been the continued need for care.

Today in its work amongst churches in local communities, all of them seeking to work more effectively with children and families in need, Müllers is still aware of the basic human need for care, security and protection. Müllers continues to care because God continues to care. But underlying the desire to care and to share the compassion of the Lord Jesus is the need to acknowledge that wholeness comes only through a relationship with Jesus. Our physical, material and emotional needs can be met in a variety of ways but Müllers believes that spiritual needs can only be met through knowing Jesus Christ. Although Müllers is not (and has never been) primarily an evangelistic organisation, everything that is done to show care is accompanied by the need to share the gospel. It is to be 'lived as well as spoken'. Many people have found faith through the unconditional love shown to them and by hearing about Jesus Christ in a non-threatening and encouraging way. The work of Müllers is explicitly Christian but it is a lovely mix of showing and sharing, acting and speaking the love and salvation of God in word and deed. The key characteristics of Müllers since the beginning have been faith, care and evangelism. In George Müller's day, he would have recognised these three elements in his ministry also:

- He lived by faith, being totally dependent on God through prayer;
- He wanted to extend the hand of love into needy young lives and care for them;
- He desired that all should have the opportunity to know Jesus Christ personally.

In George Müller's day, the Homes developed along institutional lines, and with the care of more than two-thousand children and some two-hundred members of staff, there seemed to be no other way to meet the need. Indeed very few alterations were thought to be necessary until the end of the Second World War. The introduction of the Welfare State brought about many changes in this country, and among these was the method of caring for children. As a result of the 1948 Children's Act the Trustees decided, after much prayer, to sell the five large Homes at Ashley Down. They bought, instead, smaller properties to house family groups of from ten to twelve children. It was felt that this would provide the children with a more natural environment in which to grow and with house-parents to whom they would relate.

The five Ashley Down Homes were all purchased by the local Education Authority in 1958 and they have been used continuously since then as a college campus. Today three of the buildings are being converted into flats but, because the buildings are Grade II listed, they will continue to have their distinctive appearance.

The smaller family group homes were located mostly in various parts of Bristol, Clevedon, and Weston-super-Mare. Each home had its own staff consisting of house-parents (a married couple), two assistants and some part-time domestic help. The emphasis was no longer on formal education; it was more concerned with healthy, emotional and physical development. The children attended local state schools. Most of the children came from broken homes, many were emotionally deprived in one way or another and a few were quite seriously disturbed. In many ways this new approach had been vital to meet the needs. However, the basis of the Müller Homes remained the same and it was essential for all staff involved to be

Christians. Although the nature of the Müller Homes had changed considerably since George Müller's time, the same basic principle of God meeting every need, through the power of prayer, was still the same.

In the late 1970s and early 80s, it became apparent to the Directors and Trustees of the Homes that even family group care was no longer appropriate to meet the ever-changing needs of society. Coupled with that was the fact that children were no longer coming into residential care in sufficient numbers. Local authorities and other childcare agencies preferred that the children be fostered with private families. After much discussion and prayer, it was felt that the way forward was in some way to meet the needs of *whole* families who for one reason or another were finding difficulties and pressures hard to bear.

The family group homes were replaced by day and family care, community based work and schools. In each of these areas, opportunities to show and share the love of Jesus were evident and many can testify to the quality of that care. Part of the work in the Centres was the care for young children on a daily basis, often those with mental, physical and emotional needs and to give advice and practical help to parents. They provided preventative care, play and learning opportunities. In groups of 5–10, looked after by nurses, the children had the opportunity to try their hand at cooking and painting and all sorts of creative activities. Children had the space to play, explore and develop. Parents appreciated the 'breathing space' and the genuine efforts by staff to involve them and help them in their difficulties. Parents and children joined together for special outings in the summer which were always highlights, together with the special Christmas-time activities. Many gifts of toys are received each year at Christmas-time which were invaluable in supporting families attending the Centres and are still important now as they are still available to needy families.

Referrals came from health visitors, social workers and local churches. Müllers worked closely with other caring agencies so that, together, effective help might be offered. Families themselves came for all sorts of reasons. For some, it was to make new friends or to escape for a while from cramped accommodation, or to have space for the children to play or to find help in working through difficulties such as debt problems, learning household management and cooking, sorting out marriage problems, self esteem issues or learning how to play with and relate to their children in better ways. Needs were great, especially in urban priority areas. There are so many pressures on family life to make it dysfunctional. Parents often need help to be better parents; children need to experience good quality family life.

A further development in care among children and a fulfilment of George Müller's original vision for schools was the work of the Educational Care section started in 1987. A small team of full-time school workers had the opportunity of working with some of the secondary schools in Bristol in educational care. The team sought to convey to young people in schools how the good news of Jesus Christ touches all areas of life. They went into secondary schools taking Assemblies, Social Studies, Religious Education classes and Humanities lessons and Personal and Social Education Groups. They were encouraged to see schools realising the need and relevance of introducing a Christian perspective to issues faced by young people. Many young people showed a real interest in the Christian gospel and what it had to say in their lives. Joint activities such as camps, evening and fun events were arranged among the schools. School weeks and music events, where young people could identify with what is said and sung, were seen to be very important.

It has already been mentioned that Müllers has sought to meet the challenges of the day by re-focusing its work without losing the basic foundations upon which it was founded. By the beginning of the 21st century, another major change was taking place as the Day and Family Care Centres were closed and the schools work gradually re-focused. More and more churches are reaching out into their own local communities and schools to care and to share the good news. Therefore the Directors and Trustees of Müllers felt that the time was right to finish its own direct provision for children and families and undertake a new but vitally important supportive role to help underpin that work amongst churches and other organisations. Müllers had a wealth of experience and this needed to be shared with local churches who were, and are, God's chosen vehicle for reaching a needy world.

Today Müllers is working in partnership with an increasing number of churches locally (and other Christian organisations) as they work with children, young people and families, especially the poorest. This help may be, in part, financial but mainly it is in sharing something of its experience gained over many years of child and family care to ensure that churches can offer to their local communities services that reflect best practice. So Müllers is vitally involved in networking, training, encouraging, mentoring, supervising, discipling, inspiring, sharing good practice, financing and praying. Every year Müllers trains many young people who may become the church leaders of the future. Every year lives are touched through the work of the organisation as it helps churches. Every year other Christian organisations are encouraged and supported through relationship with Müllers. Church leadership teams are challenged concerning the health and vision of the church for which they have responsibility. It is still the early stages of this development but Müllers' vision is that by 2010 there will be 100 churches (and other organisations) networked together in partnership with it, each seeking to reach out and touch the lives of many children and families in the Greater Bristol area.

The George Müller Foundation, which became the overall title for the work of Müllers in 1987, now comprises three charities, the most extensive being the Müller Homes for Children. The activities mentioned above are embraced within that charity. However, the original charity founded by George Müller and Henry Craik in 1834—the Scriptural Knowledge Institution—still sends gifts each month to Christian workers and organisations both abroad and at home. This work has grown significantly in recent years and it is wonderful to see how prayer brings together the needs of Christian workers who are living by faith and of donors seeking to give as God directs. A significant part of the amazing growth of S.K.I. has been in support of workers amongst orphans, children and families, especially through child sponsorship schemes. Although S.K.I. supports Christian workers across the spectrum of activity, work amongst children is therefore very significant and more orphans are cared for through the financial support of S.K.I. in various parts of the world today than were cared for by the orphanages, even at the high point of their operation in George Müller's day.

For many years S.K.I. ran three busy Christian bookshops in Bristol, Bath and Weston-super-Mare. These bookshops were the successors of the Bible Warehouse, also called the Bible and Tract Depot, which Müller began in 1849. However, in view of the fact that Christian bookselling had become a specialist and sophisticated activity, it was decided to sell the businesses which had traded as Evangelical Christian Literature (ECL) to Send the Light, a subsidiary of Operation Mobilization. Now these shops trade under the name of Wesley Owen.

The newest charity to be established as part of the Müller family is the Müller Homes for the Elderly (1983). Some children who were brought up and cared for at Ashley Down have found that as they grew older, they continue to be drawn to care in a home; others may have devoted their lives to missionary work and need somewhere to retire; yet others long to have a Christian environment in which to live out their final years—for them and others attracted to its clear Christian ethos, Tilsley House in Weston-super-Mare now serves as an Elderly Persons' Home providing accommodation for up to (currently) 24 and (eventually) 32 elderly residents.

When a children's home next door (Tranquil House) became available, it was purchased and converted into a number of comfortable sheltered flats with a warden. As residents get older so the advantage of being next door to an Elderly Person's Home is obvious. Now that Tilsley and Tranquil House have become established and perform such an important service for the elderly in Weston, prayerful decisions need to be made about developing this work in Bristol also.

As the Foundation seeks God for his guidance in the work amongst the elderly and children (and also amongst Christian workers worldwide), there is great confidence because God has shown himself to be faithful time and time again through answered prayer. George Müller said that he could prove that he had received 50,000 answers to prayer in his lifetime, of which 30,000 had been within twenty-four hours. Müllers continues to pray.

There are many visitors to Müller House over the year and people frequently ask whether the Foundation still follows the principles laid down by George Müller when he started the work. Many question whether a simple faith in God is adequate (or appropriate) to provide for the needs of today's complex society. The Foundation exists to re-affirm confidence in the biblical principles reflected in George Müller's initial aims expressed in the following terms:

The first and primary object of the Institution is that God might be magnified by the fact that the children under my care are provided with all they need, only by prayer and faith, without anyone being asked by me, or my fellow labourers, whereby it might be seen that God is faithful still, and hears and answers prayer.

The Foundation continues to look to God and does not fund-raise in any way, nor do we seek to declare our financial needs to anyone other than to God in prayer. This is such a crucial distinctive for the Foundation. God still answers prayer today because 'he is the same yesterday, and today and for ever'.

Today the Foundation is led by Robert Scott-Cook (Chairman) and a Board of Directors and Julian Marsh who is Chief Executive. Further information may be obtained from:

The Chief Executive,
The George Müller Foundation,
Müller House,
7 Cotham Park,
BRISTOL,
United Kingdom
BS6 6DA
Website http://www.mullers.org
E-mail: admin@mullers.org
Telephone 0117 924 5001

A small museum is open on weekdays from 10 a.m. until 4 p.m. which contains a wealth of material, both written and in photographs, concerning the work of George Müller. Visitors are warmly welcomed without advance notice but are advised to make contact, if possible, for an appointment. Similarly, an almost complete set of records concerning the former boys and girls who stayed in the Homes is available. The Foundation is in contact with many former boys and girls from the past and each year there is a reunion. Readers who would like to know more should contact the Chief Executive.

Bibliography

Autobiography of George Müller (J. Nisbet & Co.)

Roger Steer, *Delighted in God* (Hodder Christian Paperbacks)

A.T. Pierson, *George Müller of Bristol* (Ambassador, 1901)

Nancy Gatron, *George Müller and his Orphans* (Hodder & Stoughton 1963)

Fred G. Warne, *George Müller* (Pickering & Inglis)

W.H. Harding, *Life of George Müller* (Oliphants)

The Autobiography of George Müller (Whitaker House)

Answers to Prayer (The Bible Institute of Colportage Association, Chicago)

E.K.Groves, *George Müller & Successors* (Bristol, 1906)

Also literature from The George Müller Foundation

Now the Wesley Owen shop in Park Street. Müller originally bought the building for the distribution of Scriptures and tracts.

*Yours affectionately
George Müller*

George Müller

The first Wilson Street Orphan Houses

FROM PRUSSIA WITH LOVE

George Müller's house, 21 Paul Street

George Müller in his middle years

Above: New Orphan House No. 1
Below: As it is used by Bristol University today

Above: New Orphan House No. 2
Below: As it is used by Bristol University today

Above: New Orphan House No. 3
Below: As it is used by Bristol University today

Above: New Orphan House No. 4
Below: As it is used by Bristol University today

Above: New Orphan House No. 5
Below: As it is used by Bristol University today

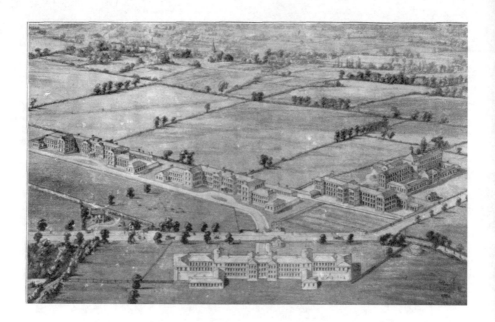

Above: Bird's-eye view of the five new orphan houses before development of the surrounding countryside

Anthony Norris Groves

Henry Craik

The first Mrs George Müller

The second Mrs George Müller

George Müller at ninety

Above: Lydia Müller and her husband at the time of their marriage
Below: George Müller's funeral procession, with orphan boys following the hearse

George and Mary Müller's grave

Chinese Whispers

The Gladys Aylward story

Carol Purves
Paperback, 128 pages
ISBN 1 903087 57 0

Wounded by a Japanese bullet as she led nearly a hundred refugee children to safety over the mountains of China, the story of Gladys Aylward is a compelling account of bravery and faith, of God's strength in human weakness. It has become immortalised through the film *The Inn of the Sixth Happiness,* starring Ingrid Bergman. This is an inspiring record of human bravery and God's sustaining power against all the odds.

A reluctant missionary

The Margaret Hayes story

Margaret Hayes
Paperback, 128 pages
ISBN 1 903087 75 9

'Go to Congo.' God's call was loud, clear and insistent. What was a recently qualified, ambitious, young nurse to make of this? She had a speech impediment; she would need more training; and where would the money for all this come from? But God was insistent, and when Margaret yielded to his will, she began an amazing journey of adventure and faith, experiencing a range of incredible difficulties and wonderful answers to prayer.

Margaret's story is a kaleidoscope of divine miracles and sheer hard work, soaring triumph and tragic loss, glorious laughter and bitter tears, spiritual reluctance and fervent courage—Brian H Edwards